Easy
Garden

Easy Garden Planning

Marjorie Willison

Illustrations by
Martin Willison

NIMBUS
PUBLISHING

Nimbus Publishing Limited
P.O. Box 9301, Station A
Halifax, NS B3K 5N5
(902) 455-4286

Design: Kathy Kaulbach, Halifax
Cover photos: Mary Primrose
Printed and bound in Canada by Best Book Manufactures Inc.

Canadian Cataloguing in Publication Data
Willison, Marjorie Jean Hanlon.
Easy garden planning
Rev. ed. of: Marjorie Willison's successful landscape design. c1989.
Includes index.

1. Landscape gardening. 2. Gardens—Design. 3. Landscape gardening—Atlantic Provinces. 4. Gardens—Atlantic Provinces—Design. I. Title. II. Title: Marjorie Willison's successful landscape design.
SB473.W535 1995   712'.6   C95-950010-3

Acknowledgements

To all the people who have helped me in the "cultivation" of this book—Thank you:

My parents, who taught me how to pull weeds and grow food in the harsh climate of Alberta.

The staff of the Halifax City Regional Library, who saved my sanity by keeping me supplied with landscape and garden books while my children were tiny.

My neighbours in Spryfield, who offered plants and old-time gardening know-how when we bought our first home.

Many keen gardeners, with their constant curiosity and passion for plants, for the many questions they have asked me on CBC Radio.

Elizabeth Eve, my friend and neighbour, who also struggles with children and a garden that need management, for her sense of humour and for suggesting that I write a book to solve our problems. As my editor, for her light and graceful hand in providing just the right finishing touch to two years of work.

Andrew Batcup, a fellow gardening enthusiast, who made astute and helpful comments on an early draft of this book.

David Lewis, also a gardener, for shedding light on a computer problem.

Bernard S. Jackson, Curator, The Memorial University Botanical Garden, for sharing his knowledge of butterflies with me.

Bob Osborne, my friend and colleague, who always finds time to answer my questions and share his expertise with me, for his down to earth suggestions for improving the manuscript.

My daughters, Meghan and Kathleen, growing along with our garden, who let me close the door and work in peace.

And my husband, Martin, who captured my ideas and brought the book to life with his drawings, for tolerating my chaos and providing the right growing conditions, year after year.

Contents

Tables

Introduction

Gardening
everywhere is
an exercise in
optimism

As a gardener's head is filled with dreams and visions for next year, even when labouring on this year's projects. Given the unique characteristics of each site, the natural and the man-made, the gardener holds the key to the secret door through which the garden's future can be seen. But the door can only be unlocked once the gardener's personal picture has been sketched. Without a design that includes not only suitable plants, but also a plan of action for the gardener, the gardening cannot begin. The best gardens are pleasant and functional, suited to the site and environment, and, most importantly, suited to the gardener.

This book is a practical guide to planning a garden, one that seeks to keep the gardener as well as the garden in mind. The gardener can plan a long or short-term strategy that will take into account needs, interests and abilities. This is a rewarding approach for homeowners, one that will yield satisfactory results and avoid the pitfalls of impractical dreams and hasty action.

The process of garden design is the same for all situations whether you have a brand new property, with little or no landscaping, or an established garden that needs some restructuring and rejuvenation, or a tiny yard or balcony garden with barely room to turn around. Firstly you analyse the site, secondly you plan the overall structure, then you choose the plants.

The analysis of the site takes into account all the present factors, the environment, the existing structures, the terrain and the vegetation, and provides the basis for a new plan. Before proceeding to the planning stage, you need to add yourself into the equation—not only what you wish, but also your capabilities and needs. The plan may proceed towards a particular focus such as outdoor living space, a wonderful view, recreation activities, or one's own secluded retreat. You might prefer a fairly open plan, or one with separate areas, full of surprises.

On a new property, for example, you might be faced with

major decisions such as whether to plant a slope to decrease erosion or terrace it to control drainage and increase outdoor living space, whether to eliminate hardpan or use it for a driveway, and whether to move large boulders or turn them into features and heat sources for tender plants.

You might be debating where to put a deck or patio and how big to make it, where to put a children's play area, where to position a windbreak and what plants to use in it, and where to position a shrub border. Questions such as these are answered early on in the book, in Chapter 1.

In an established garden you might be more concerned with rejuvenation, reducing upkeep time in a high-maintenance garden, or adapting a garden to your changing needs. After all, gardens are never finished, and half of gardening is trying something different and moving things around.

Changes in your yard or neighbourhood might bring the need for changes in your garden. Maybe a new deck has been built and you wonder how to integrate it with the house and surroundings so that it looks less like an afterthought. You might be concerned with increasing the screening in your yard to give yourself some privacy from a new house or apartment building next door.

If you have a tiny yard, or a roof garden, or are restricted to balcony gardening, you might be interested in getting more use out of a limited space, or in knowing little tricks to increase the sense of space. You will need to plan the structure carefully to get the greatest use and enjoyment out of a small space. Once the overall structure is planned, the choice of plants becomes much easier and is based on what function they serve, on the growing conditions, and on the theme or main idea of your garden. Each plant is used with a definite intention.

Lists of plants are contained in the chapters, as well as practical suggestions for actual planting. The tables in the back of the book are for easy reference to matching plants with various functions.

Perhaps you are faced with deciding whether to rip out a weedy lawn or try to rejuvenate it. You might have concerns about keeping a few flowers while phasing out a large flower border that has become too much to handle, or maybe you want drought-resistant plants to reduce watering time, or perhaps you are looking for insect and disease-resistant plants to cut down on the amount of spraying. Perhaps you have difficult growing conditions such as wet, heavy clay or thin, rocky soils, salt spray from streets in winter or seaside locations, heavy shade, or extremes of acidity or alkalinity. You might wonder if it is better to use plants adapted to extreme conditions or to adapt the conditions to suit your favourite plants.

You might have made many decisions but wonder about such details as how much topsoil to bring in, when to seed a lawn, which plants to use around the foundation of your house to reduce winter heating costs, how to choose trees for lawns, near decks, and along driveways, and what poisonous plants to avoid.

Tiny gardens need care in the choice of plants. You might know that vines are invaluable in small spaces but wonder about which ones would be best for your site. Perhaps you are keen to use container plants, but need information about proper soil mixes, suitable trees and shrubs for container growing, and grouping techniques for design and maintenance considerations. Maybe you've heard of espalier, a method of growing plants, but don't know which plants are suitable.

Tiny gardens need care in the choice of plants.

These are basic considerations when it comes to planning the structure of a garden and choosing the plants to go in it. What is even more enjoyable is choosing plants that reinforce a theme, creating a main idea in your garden. You might want to attract wildlife to your garden, or bring fragrance to a summer's evening, or make use of native plants and natural growing conditions. You might want to try your hand at edible landscaping, or make your garden alive with colour, or have it overflow with roses. Maybe you have always wanted a rockery or a peat garden or a pond.

Deciding what you want for your garden is the greatest challenge. Locating the right plants to go in it can be a challenge, too. All of the plants listed in this book have been seen growing in various zones and situations, but not all are readily available or grown in every location, nor do they attain the same size everywhere. Many worthy plants not mentioned in this book can be found in local nurseries.

The tables at the end of the book are arranged according to plant function, hardiness and size. It is no use looking for a tender, zone 6 plant at your local nursery if you live in a harsh zone 4, but you can expect to find plants hardy to zones 2, 3 and 4. Perhaps the commonest mistake in selecting plants is choosing the wrong size for a certain function. Keep in mind that plants tend to be larger in milder zones and good growing conditions than they do in harsher zones, but relative heights will remain constant. Nurseries, of course, usually sell plants that are easy to grow, so a plant that is somewhat temperamental may be difficult to locate. Some gardeners will spend years looking for just the right plant; others are perfectly content with easily found plants. A few suggestions for obtaining plants are discussed in Chapter 10.

Whatever the nature of your site, the availability of plants, and your own interests and abilities, this book is designed to help you combine these factors into a plan for a well-balanced, functional and beautiful garden.

For a full discussion of gardening methods and techniques, consult *The Complete Gardener's Almanac* (Willison, 1993). This practical month by month guide explains how and when to plant, prune, propagate and nurture a wide variety of flowers, vegetables, herbs, fruits, trees and shrubs.

CHAPTER 1

The Dream

In order for your garden to develop according to your dream there are several stages to go through.

The first stage in making your dream come true is to analyse the site and take a hard look at the restrictions it imposes and possibilities it possesses. Next is the design stage where practical considerations run side-by-side with dreams. Grading the terrain to improve drainage, for example, can open up a world of new ideas. Rocky outcrops might be incorporated into a patio design or used as a backdrop for a flower border. Windbreaks and shade trees can be planned so that they provide shelter and at the same time become part of the overall structure of the garden. The desire for recreation areas, a deck, fruit and vegetable production, play areas and a private get-away can be juggled with the storage areas and available sunshine.

These functions and desires are translated into a basic structure for your garden, one with ceilings, walls and floors forming outdoor rooms. If you feel comfortable with this level of planning, you could fine tune the plan with more aesthetic concerns. Focal points, pattern, balance, line and shape will help to capture the spirit of the garden, large or small.

After site analysis and the design stage comes plant selection which is itself broken into several stages. The most basic consideration is simply figuring out what plants are appropriate to their purpose in the garden, given the available growing conditions. This list can be focussed to include plants that reinforce a theme, such as edibility, fragrance, attracting wildlife or using native plant material. Then, if you are ready, you could consider such subtleties as shape, texture and colour of plants. You might also want to consider features for your garden—a rockery or garden seat or favourite plant. Only you can decide how much detail you want to attend to. The important consideration is to have plants that you can comfortably maintain and that are suited to the growing conditions.

Then comes the final stage of locating the plants you want and planting them in the ground. This can take place in one season or over a lifetime. It is very satisfying to work the soil, and this may explain why many people rush out with spring

fever to plant trees and shrubs without consideration to their function in the structure of a garden or without thought to the growing conditions they require. It is also very satisfying, however, to while away the winter hours or dream away a summer with planning a garden just right for you. Then you can plant with complete confidence when spring fever strikes again.

✑ Site Analysis

Whether you have a new site with your home not yet built, or an established site with a well-developed garden, a thorough understanding of the strengths and weaknesses of your holdings will bring many benefits. You will recognize how the environment, terrain and vegetation, and man-made structures interact, and how to use that interaction to plan your landscape design. This in turn will save endless effort and financial investment by giving you a clear idea of what is to be done in your planting plan. It will also help you to see your site with new eyes if you already have an established garden. The first step, though, is simply determining what you have.

The garden of your dreams can become reality by analysing the site, planning the shape of the garden, and selecting the plants. It will serve multiple needs and will mature as the users mature, always retaining its own vitality while providing its creators with the constant pleasure of interacting with it.

Environment

Environmental considerations include weather factors, hardiness ratings for your area, energy savings in winter and anything else to do with the natural environment. If you are looking for a site to build or buy a new home, for example, a south-facing slope offers shelter from winter winds and gets ample sunshine for summer gardening. A north-facing slope, on the other hand, often receives cold winter winds and little sun. Growth on a north slope is also delayed in spring, but fruit trees and early blooming plants may escape frost damage. Halfway up any slope usually offers the most shelter from winds, an ideal placement for orchard or house. Large bodies of water also affect the local environment. They keep conditions cooler in spring and retain heat in autumn, thereby moderating local temperatures.

Maybe you have noticed that one part of your house overheats in summer; a well-placed shade tree might ease this problem. As much as one quarter of heating costs can be swallowed up by wind, so you need to know from which direction most of the winter wind comes. Noting snow-drift patterns will help determine driveway placement and will indicate pockets of shelter for tender plants or outdoor living areas. Knowing where the sun shines in your yard will help you determine where to put the vegetable patch or private sun deck.

The topography of the land greatly affects growing conditions for plants. The north side of hills tend to be shady, while south-facing slopes benefit from extra warmth.

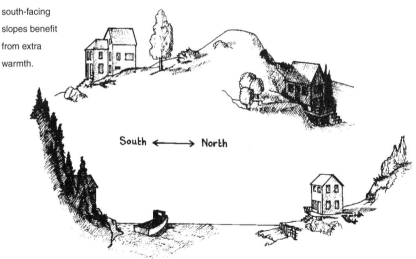

South ←——→ North

The following observations will help you pinpoint exactly what to look for around your yard in relation to the environment. Before you begin, locate your house on the lot accurately, and draw it on graph paper; 1/8 inch = 1 foot is a handy scale to use, or use an existing lot and building plan. It is not essential to use graph paper, but it helps in keeping distances accurate and in placing and estimating numbers of plants you need in the next stage. Make notes on your plan as you go through the list of factors.

Exposure to sun • Note daily and seasonal sunshine patterns throughout your lot, and pockets of heavy or dappled shade in summer. This can be checked in winter. When the moon is full and high in the sky in December, it is in the south and will give a rough indication of summer shade patterns.

Sunshine in the house • Note which rooms overheat, or are uncomfortably bright, or too dark, and for what reasons.

Winter winds • Often they are from the northwest, but local terrain and buildings can alter this considerably. Sheltered areas will be deep in snow drifts, and exposed areas will be swept clean.

Summer winds • Locate areas where you feel chilly in summer and where plants are battered about. This is especially important at coastal locations where daily breeze patterns are established by differing temperatures of the land and the ocean.

Frost pockets • Hollows, valleys, and next to tall hedges are areas where cold air settles. Clearing a plot of land in a large group of trees will often create a frost pocket.

Hardiness zone • The zone map at the end of the book shows the various zones. The lower the number, the colder and harsher the winter climate. Any plants suited to a particular zone will also grow in milder zones (those with higher numbers).

Try to orient a new house to suit the terrain and sun patterns, rather than facing the street. Look for a site or a house where most of the sunshine is in the backyard if that is where you will spend most time outdoors. Some of the preceding points may be difficult to evaluate, particularly if you haven't lived in your home for very long. It is far better to spend a year observing and planning than to rush in and make costly mistakes in your planting.

Terrain and Vegetation

Terrain can be thought of as the lay of the land, the arrangement of soil, rocks and slopes. Vegetation is any plant life on it, whether desirable or not, and ranges from towering trees to little blades of grass.

Terrain and vegetation together have a profound effect on drainage, as those with leaky basements know only too well. Groundcover is vital in control of soil erosion: roots hold soil; leaves and grass absorb the impact of rain; and plants trap eroding soil. Drainage patterns can be altered, but preserving the natural ones if they are effective is better. Damage during construction can cause severe erosion, but there are ways to minimize this.

Level areas, or lack of them, determine planting and outdoor living areas. Terrain also determines circulation routes for pedestrians and motor vehicles. There might be trees and shrubs in excellent condition on your property, or some of them might need removal. There might be huge boulders or rocky outcrops that can be turned into features or hidden behind plants. The best gardens are designed around the existing terrain and vegetation. Any changes are carried out using gentle management techniques that are harmonious with the plants, boulders and drainage patterns that are already there. The following items should help you to assess the terrain and vegetation on your property. Note your observations on your plot plan.

Rock content • If you do not see any rocks, there is probably good soil depth. Three metres is needed for a new excavation. Note depth of soil, existence of bedrock, position of boulders and rock outcrops, and potential site for a septic tank. Decide whether boulders can be easily removed or repositioned.

Slopes • Note whether all or part of your land slopes and how steep the gradient. A string level is adequate for this job.

Compaction • Locate areas of hardpan and compaction. Consider how heavy equipment, earth moving and drainage improvements might increase such problems.

Topsoil • Determine whether or not the topsoil has been stripped, and check the quality of existing soil. Take a soil sample (see page 197) and have it analysed for organic content, pH and nutrient value. If construction has not yet taken place, be sure to have the existing topsoil moved to one side and saved for your use.

Water • Note the paths that rain and melting snow and ice take to run off the property. Check downspouts and places where water collects. Soil that drains poorly will have standing water several hours after rain has stopped.

Vegetation cover • Assess condition of lawn and other groundcovers. Consider a cover crop to tide you over until a permanent planting is made.

Trees and shrubs • Note location, size and variety of existing plants, and measure canopy spread and shadow plan of trees. Look for die-back, tangled growth, damage caused by roots and tree limbs that overhang the house or outbuildings.

Food plants • Note whether vegetable plot, fruit trees and soft fruit bushes are in full or nearly full sun. Plants that bloom or fruit poorly are often too shaded or overgrown.

There is no need at this stage to make any decisions about plants; simply noting their condition is enough. Incorporating these factors into your design will be discussed in later chapters.

Structures

Structures can be thought of as the man-made elements on your property. They include the house and its arrangement of doors and windows, power and water lines on the property, storage sheds and garages, walls, fences and driveways. Outdoor living areas, such as patios and decks, and recreation and play areas are also structures in this context. Worthy of consideration at this stage are views into and out of your property and elements in the neighbourhood. Decide

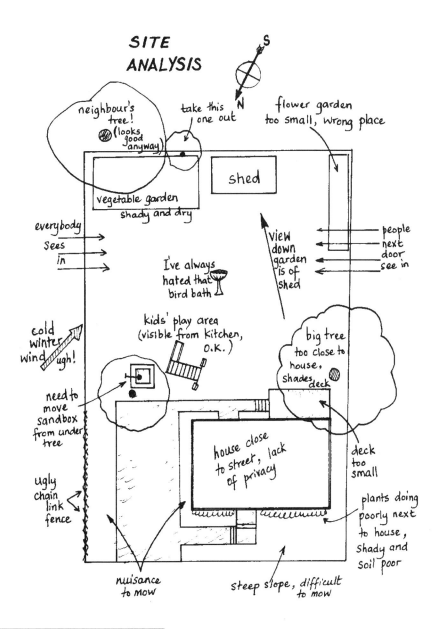

Make notes on the weather, the terrain and vegetation, and the built structures in your garden. By putting your critical needs and limitations on a plan, the garden will begin to shape itself.

whether you want to borrow from the view, blend with it, or ignore it altogether. The following items deal with structures.

House • Measure and record doors, windows and steps on your plan, and note the height of the windows from the ground.

Services • Locate water outlets, sewer and water lines, telephone poles and overhead wires. Note whether trees are causing problems with any of these services.

Overhangs • Eaves, patio cover, porch roof and carport affect sunshine, wind and rain patterns.

Outdoor living • Note location, size and condition of outdoor living areas—patio, deck, porch, recreation and play areas. Consider whether or not they are actually used by the family, and at what times of day they are or might be used.

Outdoor structures • Note condition and adequacy of walks, driveway, walls, fences, sheds, garage and parking area. Note also the amount of shade on parking and storage areas and ease of access. Consider the number of cars for the family, the daily pattern of use and need for guest parking.

Screening and barriers • Note location of pleasant views, sunrises and sunsets, unsightly features, noise, car lights and road dust. Determine short cuts of animals and people across your property.

Permanency • Consider whether you think of your house as a permanent or temporary residence. You might not want to make a large investment in landscaping a temporary residence, but some improvement in landscaping will almost certainly increase the resale value of your property.

Only an assessment of what you actually have is needed at this stage of landscape design. Once the site analysis is completed, the fun and challenge of the design stage can begin. Some of the items that gave you difficulty in the site analysis will probably become clearer as you work through a design for your garden and consider the various options.

✍ Design Stage

In designing a garden, the initial effort is towards creating a structure, a series of enclosures or rooms with ceilings, walls and floors for various functions. It is easy when designing to get so caught up in details that the overall structure is forgotten. At this stage it is enough to know that you want a windbreak, for example, without worrying yet about how tall it will be or of what plants it will be composed. Maybe you want a wall, but you needn't decide yet whether it will be a fence or a hedge. You might toy with the idea of a deck or terrace, but of prime importance at this stage is its location, not its construction or shape.

The easiest way to accomplish this is to use sheets of tracing paper over the site analysis you have completed on graph paper. With each piece of tracing paper you can try different arrangements for all the functions you want your garden to accomplish, taking into account the various environmental, landscape, terrain and plant features marked on the graph paper. It is difficult to distinguish between the various features at this stage because they are integrated. To cover the main points, the following comments might help.

Sloping property • If all or most of the site is on a slope, one or more terraces, or level areas, should be incorporated into the design. They will improve drainage of surface waters, provide level areas for construction, lawn space, recreation and planting areas, and provide circulation routes for vehicles and pedestrians. You will need enough soil to build these level areas. Coastal areas are sometimes short of soil, but rock outcrops might be usable as the backbone for terraces.

Individual slopes • If only part of the land has a steep slope, a series of smaller terraces or decks will provide level areas for outdoor rooms. Plantings can be containerized. Even on gentle slopes, different levels in the form of decks or terraces will increase the sense of space on small city lots, and will add interest to even, unbroken land. Sunken levels also create private areas protected from wind, ideal for outdoor sitting areas in windy sites.

Drainage • To prevent a leaking basement, a grade of 2% to

3% sloping away from the foundation is usually sufficient (a 2 m or 3 m drop for every l00 m). If earth moving equipment is not required, a shovel and rake might be sufficient. If erosion is a problem, try to spread drainage over a wide area. Avoid disturbing soil and vegetation on steep slopes and along the banks of water courses.

Water • A soggy area could be turned into a proper bog or planted with water-tolerant plants. Instead it could be dried out by laying drainage pipe, or built up with soil to divert the water elsewhere. Again, a 2% to 3% grade should be sufficient. Try to preserve natural drainage patterns as far as possible, or you may create more problems for yourself. Water flowing across your property could be accentuated and incorporated into the landscape design.

Rocks • Boulders, rocks and outcrops can be turned into features—as the basis for a rock garden, as part of a wall or as shelters and heat sources for plants. Boulders can make striking focal points, but imported ones almost always look contrived. Rock ledges can be used as terraces, as backdrops for plant displays, as focal points, as seats in the sun or as part of the design or surrounding shelter of a patio or deck.

Hardpan • Areas of hardpan (compacted soil) are good for driveway, parking, patio or deck, walkway, storage and utility areas. Make use of them if possible, because hardpan will have to be broken up for planting areas.

Paths and roads • Try to arrange roads, driveways and walkways to follow natural contours. If possible, avoid running driveways straight up a slope but keep them as short as possible to avoid eating up valuable yard space. Insist that heavy equipment use the planned or existing driveways as the access route during any construction. A minimum width for driveways is 2.7 m, although 3.6 m is roomier if space allows.

A turning circle requires a radius of 9 m and a driveway width of 5.5 m. Good visibility and cleared vegetation is needed at the junction with the main road.

Parking • Parking should be situated close to the main entry in a shaded area provided there is not too much messy litter from overhanging trees. A width of 11 m will accommodate 4 cars parked side by side, 12 m will accommodate 3 cars parked at a 45 degree angle, and 15 m will accommodate 2 cars parked parallel. Parking can be incorporated at the head of the driveway or along the side.

Pedestrian access • Make sure that the entrance to your property is obvious from the street. It should be bold and easily seen, and pathways should be comfortably wide for two people. Use natural walkways where possible, if adding sidewalks or constructed paths, and arrange new walkways to follow natural contours. If a path connects the driveway to the front door, it should link with where the car is parked and also be inviting for pedestrians approaching from the street.

Storage • Storage for cars, boat, trailer, garden tools and equipment, coldframes and outdoor furniture should be close to the area it will serve. Ideally, it should be positioned on the north side of the house, or in a dark or shaded area so that it does not rob the garden of valuable, sunny, growing areas.

Utility areas • Locations for garbage can, compost pile, clothesline, wood pile and so on can be screened from view, and distances to utility areas should be as short as possible. Storage and utility areas can sometimes be combined to save on space.

Outdoor sitting • Locate patios and decks in areas that are sunny or partially shaded at the time of day they will be used. People will not use outdoor living areas that are in heavy shade no matter how well planned and built they are. South or southeast locations are usually warm and sunny; southwest locations provide sunshine late in the day. Locate decks in areas sheltered from cool breezes, particularly if you live along the coast, unless your property tends to overheat in summer. Try to keep decks low, to avoid wind turbulence.

A patio or deck need not be immediately adjacent to the house; an attractive path would be an invitation to wander out to the deck. Even the front yard is perfectly acceptable, although somewhat unconventional, if there is screening of some sort around the area. A private garden enclosed with shrubs or fence will not be at all obvious from street level, and a raised terrace with a surrounding low wall will also give privacy from the street. See Chapter 4 to determine appropriate sizes.

Play and recreation • Determine how many pieces of equipment are wanted, whether the area is to be visible from the house, and from which room. A sunny or partially-shaded area is best, and it might need some fencing in. Try to have open and sheltered areas because children like little hideaways under trees and behind shrubs. You might be able to combine the play area with the deck, utility or storage areas. Space and equipment for games, sports, and swimming or wading pool should be carefully considered for practicality, frequency of use and cost. Plan for a second use when the primary function is redundant. The following court sizes for various sports may help you make the decision, but remember to add an extra 3.0 to 4.5 m all around for chairs, tables and spectators:

Decks and outdoor living areas should receive some sunshine; storage and utility areas belong in shade or where there are other poor growing conditions.

badminton . . . . 6.1 x 13.4 m
spa, hot tub . . . . 1.8 m diameter
basketball . . . . 15.2 x 28.7 m
swimming pool . . . . 5.0 x 11.0 m
croquet. . . . . 9.0 x 18.0 m
swing set. . . . . 1.8 x 3.6 m
tennis . . . . 11.0 x 23.8 m
horseshoes . . . . 2.4 x 15.2 m
table tennis . . . . 1.5 x 2.7 m
volleyball . . . . 9.0 x 18.0 m
shuffleboard. . . . . 1.8 x 15.8 m
soccer . . . . 50.0 x 100.0 m

Pets • If you have pets, decide what shelter is most appropriate, whether an exercise area is needed and what fencing is required. Some shade would be good. Again, plan for a second use.

Windbreak • If a windbreak is needed, make it long enough to shelter the house. A break in it might help to clear the driveway in winter. It will provide the greatest shelter on the leeward side to a distance of 2 to 5 times its height.

Food production • Position the vegetable patch where it will receive at least 8 hours of sunshine each day. Try to place it in a short and direct line from the kitchen, and close to a shed or garage. Determine if it will need some shelter from wind, and decide on how much time you have to plant, maintain, harvest and process food for storage. Approximately 65 sq. m is required for a family of four if extra food is to be grown for winter storage. Other food-producing plants, such as fruit trees and bushes, also need plenty of sunshine. Consider including edible plants in your landscaping plans, particularly if there is no room for a conventional orchard and vegetable patch.

Flowers • If you decide to have flowers at all, perennials require less maintenance. They are best used in conjunction with shrubs so that there is some winter interest available, or place perennial borders where they will not be seen in winter. It also helps to place flower and shrub borders parallel to the line of vision so that seasonal gaps are not so obvious. Flowers can also be located in open woods, but avoid any areas that are wet and icy in winter. Lots of light and air circulation will reduce disease and growth problems.

Allow plenty of space for a perennial border. Ideally, it should be one third as wide as it is long. A bed 4.5 m long, for example, should be at least 1.5 m wide. Most perennials have a short season of bloom, so a lot of depth is required to make a good display for an extended period. For borders longer than 12 m, aim for a width of 3 to 4.5 m. Straight borders must be rigorously maintained to look well kept, so use curved shapes for lower maintenance or an informal look.

Greenhouse and hobby areas • If there is room and sunshine enough for a greenhouse, try to orient it in a southeast or south-facing position. A greenhouse can be attached to your house, another building, or can be built freestanding. In the latter case, it might need shelter from cold winds at the back. Hobby areas such as a rose garden, birding area, herb garden, fishpond, dyer's garden and so on can be included in your garden plans.

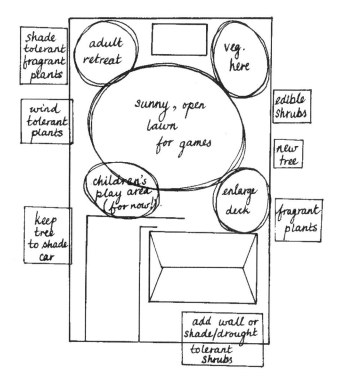

These points are broad guidelines for positioning the various functions in your garden. There is not always room for everything but you might be able to overlap some functions, such as using the driveway and parking spot for a games area, or a containerized deck planting for food production. The smaller the yard, the more carefully this phase of the planning must be done. Compromises will have to be made. You might decide, for example, to do without a windbreak in order to preserve a view. Perhaps you will choose to forgo a garage so that you can have a pond. Maybe instead, you have several options for garden arrangement and are having difficulty making a final decision. There is no right or wrong way, but the next stage might help you decide.

Once the rough garden plan is more or less in place, the structure and design can be firmed up. The plan you have sketched on paper can be built up into three-dimensional rooms with "ceilings" of trees and "walls" of fences, hedges and windbreaks. The deck area would be one room, for example, and the parking area another. It is sometimes difficult to think of the vertical dimension when planning a garden, but envisioning your plot as a room or cluster of rooms ensures that your garden has depth.

Fine-tuning the Plan

Having established the various rooms, the next step is to link them together and relate them to the whole garden. One of the characteristics of a memorable garden is its sense of unity, the feeling that all parts belong to the same garden, no matter where you wander in it. It would also probably have some feature that stands out, a tree or fountain or garden seat that is remembered long after you leave. Less obvious would be the line and shape of its various parts and its sense of balance and proportion, where no part overwhelms any other.

Aim always for simplicity. Too many elements create fuss, confusion and mess, and make small spaces seem smaller. Simplicity is also required in large gardens to help focus the

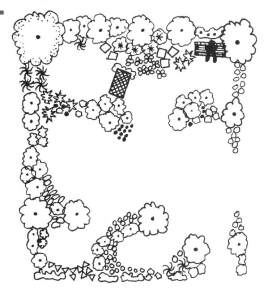

Unity is achieved by arranging the outdoor "rooms" in a hierarchy of open space. Here, several small areas open onto a larger, central area. Enclosed areas create pockets of privacy and shelter, while a carefully chosen break in the enclosure provides a sense of spaciousness and connectedness with the rest of the garden or the world beyond.

eye restfully, instead of jumping here and there in an agitated manner. There could be any number of "rooms," but keep the design simple within each one. If the plants themselves are eventful, full of colour and interest, it is best to keep adjacent areas and building materials in muted colours and uncluttered patterns. Conversely, intricate or bright elements are better offset with quiet plantings.

Unity and harmony are achieved by creating one or more enclosures, or outdoor rooms, that are related to one another and related to the house. This is most easily achieved by relating each enclosure to a larger one, and each of these larger ones to an even larger room, thus forming a hierarchy of open space. This is done instinctively, as when a patio opens onto a larger lawn. People gain pleasure from being in a small, intimate space looking out onto a larger, more open area. In a small city lot there may be room for only two or three rooms with an open lawn area being the largest room. In a large country garden, however, many small rooms can be related to larger rooms in a hierarchy until the entire garden is related to a great room beyond, the open countryside. On a lot with a very large house where there are lots of little spaces around the edges of the property but no central, open space, unity can be achieved by a series of connected rooms.

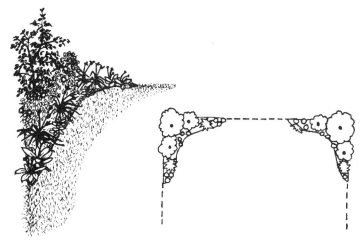

The shape of a corner planting can indicate enclosure without blocking views.

These outdoor rooms can be centred on the various functions you want in your garden, such as a play area and an outdoor seating area, and can be defined and enclosed by the windbreaks, fences and screens for which your particular garden calls. The rooms need not be totally enclosed, however. In a very open plan, each room could be merely hinted at by the use of plantings or trees at the corners. A shrub border situated in the corner of a lot, for example, could have its two ends extended slightly down the lot lines, thereby suggesting the presence of invisible walls and giving the garden a sense of enclosure without blocking it in completely. A tree planted at the corner of a lot could act as a column, much as columns are located at the corners of buildings,

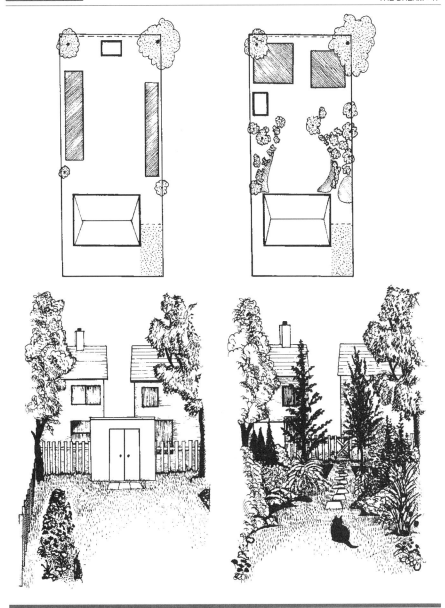

'Before'—a garden that is fully open to view, offering little variety in visual experience; 'after'—the same garden divided into two outdoor "rooms" and rich in variety despite its small size. A sense of depth and mystery has been created by the division and the path.

and the outdoor room would be quietly defined without enclosing it. Walls do not have to be tall. A knee-high hedge functions very well as a wall without being imposing.

The idea of creating unity between connecting rooms is very useful in preserving and expanding the sense of space in small gardens. A small area can actually be made to feel larger by dividing it into several rooms, much as a house that is being built suddenly feels larger inside once the inner walls go up. In lots that are long and narrow, as are so many city lots, the garden can be divided across the narrow dimension into two or more rooms. A shrub border running along one side, for example, could swing out in a generous curve, cutting the lot in two. A terrace, with a few steps up or down from another level in the garden, will unobtrusively suggest another room at the same time that it adds interest. An archway with a low fence would accomplish the same thing, and so would a path that moves from one side of a lot to the other. Anything that prevents the entire garden from being seen in one glance helps to enhance the sense of space, as long as the areas formed are interconnected.

The least desirable thing to do is to accentuate the narrowness of a lot by dividing it lengthwise, or by having a straight border or path running its length, or by filling up the middle of the space with a bed, tree or planting.

Harmonious colour schemes that are appropriate to the house, as well as smooth transitions between hard elements and plants (see Chapter 5), also help to create a sense of unity and harmony. Another way is to bond the garden with the house by relating outdoor features to the doors and windows of the house. Creating these and other areas of interest is another important principle of garden design. It is very pleasing to look out of a window or patio door at a bird bath, tree, garden seat, arbour, archway or any pleasant view, and the garden can then be built up around this line of vision, or axial line. Any feature is usually positioned at the edge of a garden rather than in the middle, where it would break up space unnecessarily.

What do you do if your line of vision from the house focusses on an unpleasant view or boring shed or runs too close to a boundary line? It is very easy to trick the eye into looking elsewhere. If vision is blocked by a mass of shrubs or a tree, for example, the eye will search out a new line of vision, which you can ensure focusses on a garden feature. Another way is to use the steps of a deck or patio to redirect the line of vision. A bond

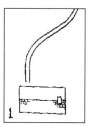

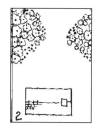

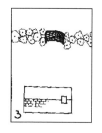

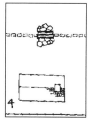

Gardens may be divided into "rooms" with the use of:

1—a path;

2—expanded shrub borders;

3—an archway and plants; or

4—steps and a change in level.

The final shape of the garden following site analysis and functional planning. It has a flowing, informal design.

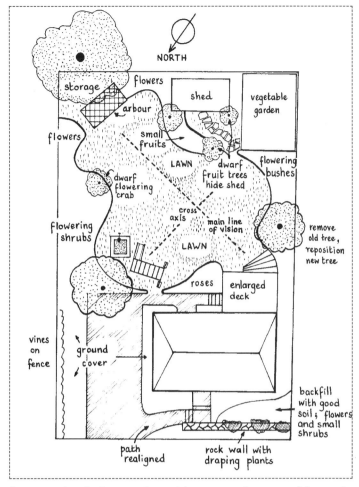

NORTH

storage
flowers
shed
vegetable garden
arbour
flowers
small fruits
dwarf flowering crab
LAWN
dwarf fruit trees hide shed
flowering bushes
cross axis
main line of vision
remove old tree, reposition new tree
flowering shrubs
LAWN
roses
enlarged deck
vines on fence
ground cover
backfill with good soil; flowers and small shrubs
path realigned
rock wall with draping plants

between the deck or patio and house can be created by positioning the steps in relation to the main window or patio door, and then turning the steps to relate to the feature or focal point. This is also an effective way of encouraging the line of vision to fan out sideways in a short, wide yard.

In a large garden, or even in a small one, a cross axis or second line of vision can be established at a right angle to the first. This could focus on a second feature in another room that opens off the first room, following the established hierarchy.

Once you have a rough idea of how you want the rooms in your garden arranged, you could firm up the design by drawing in shapes of shrub borders, hedges, fences and so on. You will probably find yourself using either formal or informal lines, depending on your personal preference.

Formal designs are symmetrical, with one side a mirror image of the other, and they have sharp, clear, regular angles in their makeup. They are based on patterns that are square, circular, oval, rectangular, or diagonal. Only one shape would be used, but it would be repeated all over the garden. A design based on a circle, for example, might have a circular pond, a deck with a semi-circular edge and steps, round flower beds, round paving stones in a path or sidewalk, and so on. Formal designs demand a lot of maintenance to keep them looking trim and are less popular now than years ago.

Informal layouts, on the other hand, are easier to maintain. They need not be based on a regular shape, and the lines can be free flowing. They help to soften the harsh, architectural lines of a house. One thing to watch for is that the curves do not become too exaggerated. Lines that look smooth and sweeping on paper can look fussy and squiggly when viewed at eye level on the ground, and they can be very difficult to mow. A way around this is to use a garden hose to lay out your beds and borders. That way you can play around with all kinds of curves until you find the one that pleases you. Try running a lawn mower along your planned curve to ensure that curves are not too sharp for easy mowing.

If you have a house that is symmetrical, you could choose a formal or informal layout, but it is next to impossible to successfully impose a formal layout beside an asymmetrical house. You could, if you like, have a formal layout close to the house and ease into a less formal layout further away. Whatever you choose, the lines should be pleasing and attractive to you.

This is also the time to look for balance in your design. If you have a large deck, for example, you could balance it with a tree or substantial shrub border opposite it. If you have a small feature such as a garden seat, it could be balanced with a single shrub. South-facing borders can be wide and generous, north-facing ones less so, but they should both be balanced with a tree or something equally substantial on the opposite side of the garden. Proportions should be appropriate, too, with trees, hedges, borders and so on in scale with the size of the house and yard.

Some people have an almost instinctive grasp of these principles, others learn it. Incorporating these ideas into your landscape design will result in a functional and attractive garden when built up according to the ideas which follow.

Various shapes can be used creatively in subtle ways. An oval lawn, for example, can be used to make a small garden appear larger because viewers think they are seeing a circle in perspective. Seating areas based on a circle, square or hexagon are rather static, but those based on a rectangle or oval give a sense of calm without feeling too static.

Ceilings

So often in landscape design the vertical dimension is forgotten. Working to incorporate a ceiling of some sort in a design will ensure that a garden is not flat and static.

A ceiling in a garden might be a spreading tree, the roof of a patio, an arbour or a vine-covered trellis. On a balcony or tiny patio, a ceiling might be a graceful vine or a few potted plants hanging overhead. Whatever its form, a ceiling can give a feeling of enclosure, provide shade and protection or screen from overhead viewers. A large tree providing a ceiling might also be the focal point in a garden; and an arbour facing a shrub border gives balance and weight to a landscape design.

Constructed Ceilings

If you have a small lot, there probably isn't room for a spreading tree, but you can accomplish many objectives with inanimate structures and vines. On a deck or patio, for example, where you want a sense of partial enclosure, some protection from the elements and some screening from overhead viewers, a clear plexiglass roof with vines scrambling over it or pots of flowers and foliage hanging from it will accomplish all three with minimal use of space. Be aware that an opaque overhang projecting from a house will shade the windows. In winter deciduous vines drop their leaves, letting in more light, but evergreen vines might become a problem.

A small yard with little room for a tree might be well served by a free-standing structure. The only sunny area in the yard suitable for a deck might be some distance from the house, so a light and airy arbour that lets in lots of sunshine might be the answer. The roof could be partially enclosed, or completely covered with plexiglass, or formed of open latticework. Both closed and open structures give a sense of enclosure, so what you choose depends on how you plan to use a particular outdoor room. It is best situated at the edge or corner of a lot so that space is not unnecessarily broken up.

Add a vertical component to the garden by creating "ceilings," such as an arbour.

There are excellent, readily available do-it-yourself manuals on outdoor structures. Keep in mind, though, that even open structures are heavy, especially if covered in vines. Get professional advice if you are at all uncertain about support structures or any part of the construction process. Even if you hire a professional, it is worthwhile reading up on outdoor structures to give you a clearer idea about what kind you want.

✣ Trees as Ceilings

If there is no room on your lot to plant a tree but a neighbour's tree reaches into your yard, by all means incorporate this tree into your own design. It might form a den of dappled shade ideal for a cozy seat or an outdoor dining-area.

If you decide that your yard is really incomplete without a tree of some sort, and you have the space, you will want to know what that tree is to accomplish so that you can choose the tree most suited to your needs and position it wisely. Choice of trees is also very much determined by their ultimate height and width. If you already have trees and are considering removal of some, you will need to determine if they are an appropriate size and serve an appropriate function.

Trees for Shading

Deciduous trees that form the top layer of the plant canopy are ideal for providing shade; evergreens are the wrong shape for that and function better as walls. Deciduous trees, however, vary considerably in their branching structure and the size and density of their leaves. This, in turn, determines the density of the shade they cast, from lightly dappled shade for outdoor living spaces to quite dense shade for cooling houses in summer. Shade that is too dense, though, is not conducive to good lawn growth or outdoor living, and light shade won't do much to keep a house cool.

In placing a tree to shade a house, west or south walls are best protected because they get the hot afternoon sun. When the tree is tall enough it will also help to shade the roof. Observe the height of the sun in summer and again in winter to see the difference in the sun's angle. This should help you to place a tree to get maximum shade in summer and maximum sunlight in winter. The advantage of deciduous trees for shading is that they lose their leaves in winter, although densely-branched trees such as oaks and maples can block out nearly as much sun when bare as they do when in leaf. Any of the larger lawn or specimen trees that cast medium to dense shade can be used, although fastigiate or upright varieties would not be your best choice if shade is what you want.

If possible, position large shade trees towards the corners, or at least the edges, of a small property to act as columns to your outdoor rooms.

A well placed deciduous tree will block out hot summer sun yet let in warming rays when the sun is lower during winter.

Feature Trees

Sometimes a tree is desired for its beauty. You might long to look out the window and see a tree in all its seasonal glories, or there might be a gap in your landscape that seems to cry out for a tree. If this is so, it might work out that you can place a tree to do double duty. A breakfast nook that gets squinty-eye sun in the morning might lose its view if curtains are hung, but a small tree outside the window would filter the sun and be a joy to view every day. A small specimen tree would also help to screen a living-room window from the street without resorting to tall, heavy hedges on the boundary. Some trees are better than others as specimen trees (see Table 1), either because of their shape or because of more attractive characteristics (see Chapter 9).

Small to large coniferous trees, depending on the space available, can also be used as specimens and are particularly effective in the winter landscape (see Table 2).

Trees can also be used to frame a feature, such as a large body of water. They can be planted on each side of the view, giving a well defined picture, or they can be planted sparingly in front of the lake or ocean, providing a lacy screen while protecting from wind off the water.

Street and Driveway Trees

You might discover that the ideal place for a tree in your landscape is just beyond your front door on public property. If this is the case, check with the municipality to see if they will permit you to plant a tree there, or ask if they will plant one and take the opportunity to choose one of your own liking.

Larger trees are better suited to wide streets and country lanes, and smaller ones to quiet neighbourhoods and farm lanes. It is a concern to see towns and cities planted predominantly with one kind of tree, such as maples, and only a few other species. As a health measure, to prevent the spread of insects and disease, it is a good idea to have no more than 5% of any one species in an area, and no more than 10% of any one genus. Planners, of course, choose trees that are pest and disease resistant and that withstand urban conditions. If most of the trees are the same, a new pest or disease can destroy most of a community's trees. By all means choose some trees that are not so common, not just for street planting but for your own yard as well.

Trees for Deck or Patio

Near a deck or patio or any other outdoor room, a tree is usually chosen more for screening or enclosure than for the shade it casts. For optimal screening, the positioning of a tree is more important than its size.

In planting a tree near a patio or deck, try to position it at or near a corner. Columns in a constructed outdoor room are placed at corners, and trees can assume this function if they, too, are positioned at corners. If you already have a tree and are building a deck, try to position the corner of the deck near it. Of course, if that is not feasible, you can build the deck around the tree and make it a feature. Columns or trees, whatever their position, are ideal places for sitting, leaning and enjoying the fragrance of the flowers. See Table 1 for patio trees.

⊰ Spacing and Arranging Trees

How you space and arrange trees depends on what function they are to serve, the size of the yard and the size of the tree. A tiny lot or balcony garden might allow one small flowering tree growing in a container. Small lots might have room for one shade tree and two, or at most three, small flowering trees. A larger lot, say 30 m to 50 m wide, might have room for two large shade trees and five small flowering trees. Large trees are those that tower over a two-storey house; medium trees would be as tall as a two-storey house and small trees are shorter and possibly shrub-like.

Sometimes a single tree can create a ceiling for more than one outdoor room such as when its branches stretch out over a deck and a nearby driveway or parking spot. The size of the house and yard and the size of the tree must be in scale, of course, and it might be better to choose two or three small trees instead of one big one if you have a small lot. It is also wise to check on what is growing in your neighbours' yards. Check to make sure there isn't a young tree just the other side of the fence from where you plan to put yours.

Small trees can be planted as close as 3 m to 6 m from the house, medium trees from 7 m to 10 m, and large trees from 10 m to 15 m away. This will keep branches far enough away to prevent damage to roof and walls and will also keep roots a safe distance from foundations. These distances are also good guidelines for spacing between trees, although trees of the same variety can be planted closer together.

Sometimes you might want to plant a few trees to create a shaded woodland area, or you might already have a wooded area that needs some thinning or changing in various ways. Thin the trees according to the suggested spacing. To create maximum shade under a group of trees, position them so that the wider side of a group of, say, three trees faces south.

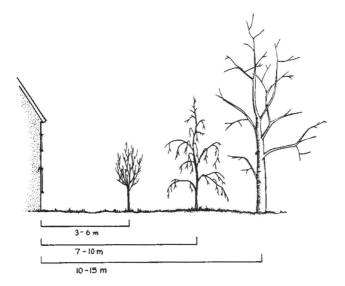

Plant trees well away from buildings to prevent damage to roofs and foundations. The larger the mature size of the tree, the greater the distance.

In any cluster, it is more pleasing to look at an odd number of trees. It is also better to arrange them so that they are not evenly spaced. This looks more natural and informal, and if one dies or becomes diseased, it can be removed without leaving an obvious gap. As well, if trees are evenly spaced they look more formal, and one is inclined to look for uniformity in size and shape which is almost impossible to achieve.

Once you have decided where to position your trees, take one last look up to make sure there are no utility wires overhead!

✐ Maintenance

The size of trees is very important in considering maintenance. So also are rate of growth and depth of the roots.

Very large trees drop more leaves, are far more difficult or impossible for the home gardener to prune and can cause considerable damage if they are broken or damaged in a storm. On the other hand, they tend to live longer.

Trees that grow very quickly are sometimes short lived, necessitating removal and replacement. Birches, Catalpa and

Allow plenty of room for the movement and growth of trees when they are incorporated into decks.

Poplars fit this category. Trees that grow quickly also tend to be more easily storm damaged. They have the advantage, though, of filling in a landscape quickly, and this is important for impatient gardeners, for gardeners in temporary residences, or for situations where immediate shelter from wind is required.

Large trees that grow quickly and that are also longer lived include Green and White Ash, American Linden (Basswood), White Willow, White Maple and Red Oak. Medium-sized trees that grow quickly include Amur Cork, European Mountain Ash (Rowan), Horse Chestnut and Honey-Locust.

A lot of the smaller trees, such as Russian Olive, Sumac, Japanese Tree Lilac and Hawthorn, grow at a moderate rate and a few, such as Hop-Hornbeam (Ironwood), Fringetree, Weeping Purple Beech and Japanese Maple, grow quite slowly. One advantage to this is that they never seem to outgrow their allotted space.

One potentially very large tree, Ginkgo, is so slow growing that some gardeners are convinced it never grows at all, and for this reason it is often treated as a medium-sized tree.

Trees that are shallow-rooted or invasive can also create increased maintenance by growing into drains or causing poor growing conditions for other plants over the root zones. These would include such trees as American Beech, Weeping Willows, White Willow, Norway Maple, Birch, Cherry and Poplars.

If you have only shallow soil, choose smaller trees that won't be uprooted in a storm.

If you particularly want shrubs under trees, choose shrubs that tolerate poor, dry, somewhat shaded conditions. It is a constant battle to keep the shrubs supplied with enough moisture and nutrients because, without help, the shrubs are nearly always out-competed by the tree. It also helps a great deal to choose deep-rooted trees such as Hackberry, American Linden (Basswood), any of the Oaks, Ginkgo, Butternut and Tulip Tree. A wider variety of shrubs can be planted beneath them because the tree roots are deeper in the soil than most shrub roots. Smaller, deep-rooted trees include Bradford Callery Pear, Saucer Magnolia and Chinese Chestnut. Most of the small flowering trees are shallow-rooted, but they don't seem to create problems because there is much less tendency for gardeners to plant shrubs underneath them.

If you want to plant a tree in your lawn, be sure to choose one with which your grass can live. In general, deep-rooted trees that cast only light to moderate shade seem to make the best lawn trees. Stay well away from Norway Maple, Beech, Poplar, Weeping Willow and Black Walnut trees. That way, your lawn will be a pleasure and not a battle ground between you and the tree. Many of the specimen trees listed in Table 1 can also be planted in your lawn, but you might want to use mulch or ground covers under them if they are not compatible with lawns.

> Consider the depth of rooting when deciding what kind of trees to plant.

❧ Moving, Removing and Rejuvenation

You may be in the situation where there are already trees on your property, but you wonder about moving them to a better location, thinning selectively, rejuvenating them, or whether some of them are even worth saving. Maybe you wish you could just cut them all down and start all over. Before doing anything drastic, consider the various options.

If you have small, young trees in potentially bad positions too close to your house you might be able to move them. Ideally, you would root prune one growing season before you plan to move them, either in the autumn or the following spring while they are dormant. Spring is usually recommended, unless you keep the trees carefully watered and protected from winter winds.

To root prune, dig a narrow trench the depth of a spade in a circle around the tree. Locate the trench at a distance of 12 times the diameter of the trunk. This guideline should help gardeners to be realistic in the sizes of trees they attempt to move. The same method can be used for trees from the wild, keeping in mind that trees should certainly be no more than 2 m tall, and 1.5 m or less is even better. Evergreens should be even smaller. In the wild, tree roots can run for quite some distance, so root pruning is especially important. Larger trees grown in the excellent conditions of a garden can also be moved because of a more compact root ball.

Dig rootball with a radius that is 12 times the diameter of the tree trunk.

If you have large trees in poor positions, you might be able to have some of them moved by experts, for a small fortune. In reality, however, you are probably faced with three choices: put up with them, cut them down, or do some pruning.

If you have a particularly fine specimen, for example, you might decide to leave it in place, even though it is too close to the house and its roots are ruining the patio surface. If a tree with similar drawbacks is showing signs of dieback or is not attractive to you, the decision to cut it down is much easier. It takes a long time to grow a tree, and the decision to cut it down is often difficult, but it makes no sense to live with a problem or with someone else's mistake.

Pruning, though, can often alleviate tree problems without making drastic changes in the landscape. The tree that is too close to the house, for example, can have the large branches over the roof removed so that a storm won't bring them crashing down on your house. If roots are threatening the foundation, they can be pruned by digging a trench between the tree and house, and then backfilling with the same dirt. The tree next to your deck or patio that casts dense shade, making sitting outdoors uncomfortably cool or dark, might benefit from having the crown thinned. An expert should probably be called in to do this. You might also consider removing the lowest branches. If the trunk of a large tree is cleared of branches up to a height of 8 m to 10 m, a lot more light and sunshine will reach the ground underneath the tree without destroying its shape and function.

It might be that the trees themselves need thinning out, rather than, or in addition to, pruning of individual trees. Keeping in mind the recommended spacing for trees, you might solve a lot of your problems by selectively removing entire trees, taking out the aged and diseased ones and removing some of the crowded saplings. This will open up your landscape considerably without creating scars and can also be used to change the view or shift the emphasis in your yard. If you are forced to remove trees during construction, try to remove only crowded, dying and otherwise undesirable trees. Avoid burying the stumps because they will eventually rot, and covering soil will settle.

Sometimes a tree that you like is in a reasonably good position and you want to keep it, but it doesn't look very healthy. In this situation, every effort should be made to restore the health of the tree. Insect and disease problems should be investigated and remedied, dead and diseased branches removed and bark damage repaired. Cut branches off just above the branch collar, almost flush with the trunk or adjoining branch, because stubs do not heal properly. Damaged bark should be cut with a sharp knife to a rounded diamond shape.

One of the surest ways to destroy a tree is to use a lawn trimmer nearby. If you use one of these tools and your tree is ailing, check the bark at lawn level for any signs of damage. Clean the ragged edges of the bark with a sharp knife and either repair the damage with bridge grafting, or wrap the trunk in a tree guard to prevent further damage. In either case, remove some of the turf and spread a mulch under the tree.

To further rejuvenate your tree, spread a layer (2.5 to 5 cm) of compost or rotted manure over the root zone

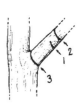

incorrect   correct

Bark cannot heal over properly if stubs are left on the tree after limb removal. Use three pruning cuts to avoid tearing the bark, and make the last cut just above the branch collar.

each spring, or mulch with a layer of leaves or shredded bark. If this is not feasible, say for street trees, apply fertilizer, and lime if required, in late autumn. Use 870 g of 10-6-4 fertilizer per 1 cm diameter of the trunk, 60 cm above the base. For fruit trees, use 9-5-7 fertilizer. Pour the fertilizer into holes that are 20 cm to 40 cm deep and 0.5 m to 1 m apart just outside the drip line of the tree. For large trees, punch another row of holes 0.5 m to 1 m inside the first circle and continue in this manner until the outer two-thirds of the tree is fertilized. A mulch of compost or leaves is usually sufficient fertilizer.

Providing the right growing conditions is the best way to keep trees healthy.

Trees that are in stressful positions, such as street trees, and trees that require a lot of moisture, such as birch trees, should be watered deeply and generously every two weeks. Pests such as the bronze birch borer are much less likely to attack trees that are healthy and free of stress.

Many times the problems that trees are having can be related to the soil. Soil compaction over the root zone, say under a driveway or where heavy equipment has been working, can spell the death of a tree. So too can extra soil added over the root zone. So often in new homes where a lot of earth has been moved, or in older homes where topsoil has been brought in, roots are smothered to death and the tree dies slowly over a period of years. According to Agriculture Canada, the trees most likely to suffer from an additional layer of soil are: Maple, Beech, Dogwood, most Oaks, Pine and Spruce. Somewhat less susceptible are Birch, Cedar (Thuja) and Hemlock. Least likely to suffer are Elm, Poplar, Pin Oak and Locust. As well, a few centimetres of clay soil are much more damaging than gravelly or sandy soils. If more soil must be added for grading purposes, or if soil must be removed around a tree, a tree well can be built.

Sometimes a good tree in the right position is having health problems because the soil itself is not suited to the tree. Trees adapted to dry, sandy soils will not do well in heavy, wet clays, for example, so one is left with the choice of removing the tree and planting a more appropriate one, or changing the soil. Improving soil drainage will often work wonders without going to the extreme of removing the tree or changing the soil. Working in lots of well rotted manure and compost will also improve both sandy and clay soils.

Because trees represent a major feature and investment in a landscape, it is worth your while to make every effort to preserve your trees and keep them in good health. The ceiling they create forms the basic structure and sets the tone of your garden and is a legacy to the gardeners who follow you.

CHAPTER 3

Walls

alls in gardens come in a wide variety of forms and serve many functions. They may be living walls of trees and shrubs, constructed walls such as fences and brick walls, or combination walls such as planted stone walls and espaliered plants against a fence. The functions served by walls, however, are related more to height than to composition of the walls.

Knee-high walls help to give direction, such as a hedge or flower border along a path or walkway. They suggest gently and unobtrusively which way a visitor is welcome to walk. They are also a good height for sitting, such as a wall around a deck or terrace.

Waist-high walls make a stronger statement about directing traffic and forming barriers to keep out invaders. They also create a sense of partial enclosure. You might, for example, want to set apart the deck or patio area from the rest of the garden while still maintaining a feeling of openness.

Chest-high walls create a clear sense of enclosure and form very definite boundaries without obstructing view. These are often used at the edges of properties as hedges or fences, or as shrub barriers next to a cliff or a steep slope overlooking a fine view. Head-high walls or taller are needed to screen out undesirable views or create privacy from neighbouring buildings and gardens. They needn't be excessively tall because strategic placement is more important than size.

The heights of walls determine their function: 1—knee-high walls give direction; 2—waist-high walls give a sense of partial enclosure; 3—chest-high walls form boundaries; and 4—head-high walls act as screens.

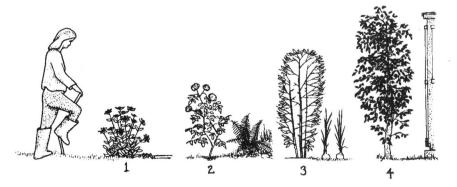

1   2   3   4

Walls that are intended as windbreaks vary considerably in height, from low fences or shrubs that shelter vegetable patches to towering trees and thick shelter belts that act as windbreaks for large areas and tall buildings. Their height depends as well on what other functions they serve, whether as barriers or screens or partial enclosures.

Scale plays a part, too, in sizes of walls. Large properties need taller and wider barriers and screens than tiny, intimate lots. A vine-covered trellis seems perfectly in scale for enclosing a small property, but a wide, generous shrub border or massive hedge is more appropriate on a large property.

Once the desired function and size of garden walls have been determined, more detailed decisions can be made about their composition. You might want to consider constructing terrace walls if your land is steeply sloped, or decks and fences if your lot is small, or a combination of careful grading and shrub borders for a natural, lush look.

Both the cost and the gardener's abilities are important considerations in deciding what kinds of walls will be used. Someone skilled in carpentry might choose to build a fence, whereas someone else, skilled in plant propagation, might plant a hedge.

Walls may be made up of plants or constructed materials. This garden shows a knee-high sitting wall; a waist-high wall of plants that partially encloses the vegetable garden; a constructed, chest-high fence that defines the boundary of the garden; and a tall wall of plants that screen the view and provide shelter from wind.

Growing conditions come into play, too, in making decisions. It might be easier to cover an existing chain-link fence with attractive vines than to replace or improve poor, rocky soil in order to grow a beautifully manicured hedge in the same place.

In order to make the decisions most appropriate to your needs and abilities consider each of the various types of walls.

৶ Living Walls

Plants appeal because they put us in touch with nature. They are part of the earth and help to integrate our homes and buildings with the surrounding landscape. They tune us in to the changing seasons and bring us an abundance of food and beauty. In return, they may need watering, fertilizing, a little or a lot of pruning, and anywhere from a minimal to a considerable investment in money, time and energy.

In deciding between evergreen and deciduous plants for various situations, several characteristics should be considered. Growth rate might be important to some gardeners. If you think of your home as a temporary residence, or are anxious for rapid growth to cover an eyesore, you may opt for generally cheaper, faster-growing deciduous plants. They tend to be shorter lived and need more pruning. In a permanent home, and with no sense of haste, you may choose more expensive, slower growing evergreen material or choice deciduous plants.

Coniferous evergreens tend to be expensive and more prone to breakage in heavy snow storms, but they make better windbreaks, afford better privacy, and look more attractive in

A mature wall of plants of various heights has blended together to accommodate several functions and uneven topography.

winter. Evergreens make good backdrops, too, for a selection of deciduous shrubs. They tend to be dark and heavy, so they form strong structural elements in the landscape. This can be tempered somewhat by using lower heights. Broad-leaved evergreens, such as Hollies and Rhododendrons, have much the same advantages and disadvantages as coniferous evergreens, except that some of them produce flowers and fruit, and they must be sheltered from winter winds.

Deciduous shrubs, on the other hand, are usually far less costly, especially as they can be easily propagated by the home gardener. They are also less likely to break in snow storms, and they bring considerable interest to gardens with their variety in leaf colour, sequence of bloom, fragrance, berry production, and fall coloration. Some are also attractive in winter, particularly those with coloured twigs and unusual outlines. They are lighter in appearance than evergreens, especially if unpruned, so they form lighter-duty structural elements.

A hedge is a living wall made up of one kind of plant; a shrub border contains several kinds of flowering shrubs; and a windbreak, another type of living wall, is composed of wind resistant plants. Certain plants which form walls are better suited to some functions than to others.

Hedges

For hedges or any boundary planting an important consideration is the amount of space available. If your neighbour agrees, a hedge can be planted on the boundary line and so take up less space in your own yard. If not, your hedge must be planted inside the boundary line one-half the distance of its ultimate spread. A hedge 2 m wide, for example, would then be planted 1 m inside the boundary line.

Hedges are also used as dividers and screens on your property. Formal hedges are half as wide as they are tall and need clipping two to three times a year. Informal hedges, on the other hand, need only a light pruning once a year and form better windbreaks but are fully as wide as they are tall. They are also effective as screens and are often used in naturalized settings. Some shrubs look better as informal hedges; others are suitable as either formal or informal hedges.

In Table 2 several of the shrubs are listed in more than one height category. The higher category is the plant's ultimate,

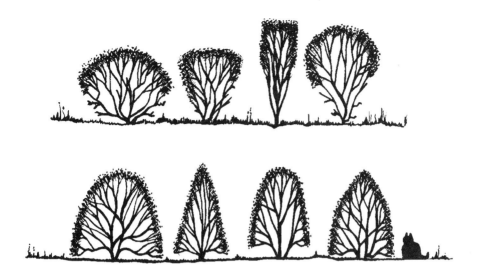

untrimmed or lightly trimmed height, whereas the lower height is that to which the plant can easily be kept with regular pruning.

Upright coniferous evergreens tend to be either columnar or pyramidal. Columnar genera, such as Junipers, Cedars *(Thuja)* and False Cypresses *(Chamaecyparis)*, are useful for a hedge intended as a screen or for tight spaces. Typically pyramidal shapes, such as Fir, Spruce, Yew and Hemlock, help to define space and are best used as border or boundary hedges.

As an approximate guide to cost and spacing of plants, knee-high hedges are usually planted with one plant every 30 cm, waist or chest-high hedges with one plant every 50 cm, and tall or informal hedges with one plant every 70 cm. A narrow hedge would have plants arranged in a straight row, and a large or informal hedge would probably have the plants staggered. Be sure to strip, chop up and bury the sod when digging a trench to plant a hedge. This will add organic matter and eliminate competition from weeds and grass while the young shrubs are getting established. Working rotted manure or compost into the soil also adds valuable organic matter and helps plants withstand dry periods.

It is a good idea, whether your hedge is formal or informal, to cut back all deciduous plants to the same height as the shortest one at planting time. If you don't, the shortest one never catches up with the taller ones; in addition, cutting back the plants eventually produces a denser growth.

If you have an established hedge and aren't happy with the way it looks or wonder if it is serving any useful purpose, you might ask yourself a few questions. Does it seem the right height, or is it so tall that it seems to close in on you? Is it serving as a windbreak for you or your neighbour? Large snowdrifts on one side or the other indicate that it is; this could be a disadvantage next to a driveway. Does it screen out a desirable view, or would cutting it lower give you less privacy? Is it healthy and green on top but bare at the base? If so, it has probably been improperly pruned in the past and needs to be rejuvenated.

Screens

A living screen may be a strategically placed shrub, or a tall boundary hedge that doubles as a screen, or a simple clump of trees. The main consideration in screening is deciding exactly what you want to block from view or from what you want to be screened. Then you juggle available space and growing conditions and any particular plant characteristics you desire.

A large shrub or small tree is as effective a screen when placed close to the viewer as a large tree placed some distance away.

The sketch below illustrates how a small shrub close to the viewer can be as effective at screening as tall plants placed further away. If you are uncertain about the heights you need, play around with poles of varying heights stuck into the ground in various positions.

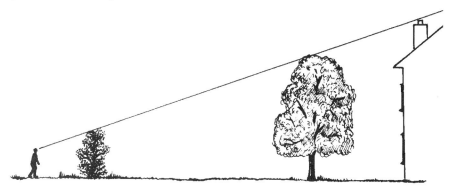

Sometimes a single, multi-trunked tree can be an effective screen. Such trees would include:

Alternate-Leaf Dogwood	*Canoe(Paper)Birch*
Mountain Maple	*Amelanchier*
Caragana	*Purple-Leaf Sandcherry*
American Hornbeam	*Gray Birch*

Saucer Magnolia   *Amur Maple*
Japanese Maple   *Silver (White) Birch*
Angelica Tree   *Japanese Tree Lilac*

Flowering Crabapples can easily be made into multi-trunked trees. On any young tree with a caliper of 2 cm or less, cut off the tree about 5 cm above the ground. Several 1 m stems will grow and all but the best three or five should be removed.

Sometimes it is not sights but sounds that have to be screened out. It would require an enormously wide band of vegetation to effectively screen sound, but even a narrow hedge can be a very good psychological barrier. Not seeing the cause of the noise somehow helps to distance us from the sound.

Plants used as screens are spaced apart two to four times the distances used for tall hedges.

Windbreaks

The size and composition of windbreaks depends on the size of the area to be sheltered. A windbreak may range from a single row of vegetation sheltering a vegetable patch to a wide shelter belt with several rows of evergreen and deciduous material sheltering several hectares.

It is often the northwest side of a house that requires shelter, but check local conditions. Land features and buildings can alter wind direction considerably, and storms often blow in from the south. The greatest shelter occurs behind a windbreak two to five times the height of the windbreak. If the windbreak has to be planted fairly close to a house, it is best planted at a distance of three to five times the height of the windbreak. If it is any closer, the house will be buried in snowdrifts, and any further away will give less than maximum protection. The windbreak must also be long enough that it shelters a sufficient area. A strategically placed gap in a windbreak can sometimes clear a driveway of snow in winter. On winding roads, or where a driveway is broadside to the wind, trees should be set back 20 m to 25 m from the road.

Coniferous evergreens have long been regarded as ideal windbreaks, but not all evergreens are equal in this regard. What is desired is tall, narrow, dense evergreens with branches to the ground. Pine and Fir grow quickly, but after a few years they lose their lower branches. Spruce, Hemlock and

Cedar are dense and hold their branches to the ground, but Hemlock and Cedar cannot withstand harsh winter winds. They might be good for windbreaks in some urban settings, as are some of the upright Junipers. That leaves Spruce as the best windbreak plant, but only in situations where it can grow to a large size.

Some deciduous plants are also good as windbreaks (see Table 2). They have the advantage of growing quickly and, if planted close together, can form a tight windbreak. As a rough guide to distances, the shorter ones up to 2 m tall should be placed 60 cm apart, the intermediate ones up to 3 m tall about 1.2 m apart, the tall ones of 6 m or more about 2 m apart, and very tall plants about 2.5 m to 3.0 m apart. Similar spacing can be used for evergreens. The aim is to filter wind and slow it down, not to create a solid wall which would increase turbulence. Growth in such tight conditions will be limited by competition, so ensure an ample supply of manure or compost at planting time, and a steady supply of moisture for the first two or three years until established.

Evergreens and deciduous plants can be used in combination as well. The spacing between plants would be the same, and the plant material within each row would be of one kind, but there would be two or more rows of different plants. The rows would be spaced about 4 m apart, with the trees in alternate rows staggered.

A three-row windbreak, for example, could have a first row of white spruce on the windward side, a middle row of fast growing deciduous trees, and a third, inner row of flowering trees or shrubs. A very large windbreak might have two rows of spruce, a row of deciduous trees that grow quickly, another row of slower growing, longer lived deciduous trees, a row of flowering trees, and a final, inner row of flowering shrubs. Composition and size of the windbreak depends very much on how much space is available and the size of the area to be sheltered.

Shrub Borders

A shrub border containing several kinds of flowering trees and shrubs, often with a background of evergreens, can serve many functions. You might use one as a partial enclosure around a patio, as a screen in front of a neighbour's compost heap, as a boundary marker, or simply as a large planting to give balance to your landscape design. For example, a shrub border might balance a large tree or deck or arbour in the opposite corner of a yard.

In locating a shrub border, it is good if you can have it curving outwards in a southerly direction. Its back would be towards the north, and the main body will get ample light. If you choose to locate a border facing north, it seems more fitting to make it narrower and less lavish, although you certainly will be able to locate plants suited to shady conditions.

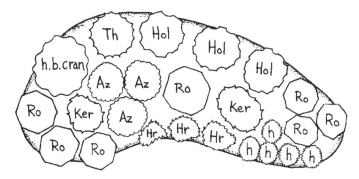

A large shrub border planned for the different seasons: for winter interest, *Thuja* (Th.), *Holly* (Hol.) and *Kerria* (Ker.); for spring bloom, *Heaths* (h), *Kerria* and *Azaleas* (Az.); for summer, hardy shrub *Roses* (Ro.); and for autumn colour, *Highbush Cranberry* (h.b. cran.), recurrent-blooming *Roses* and *Heather* (Hr.).

In its simplest form, a shrub border is simply a collection of individual plants. It is a fairly straightforward exercise to place evergreens and larger deciduous plants at the back, and intermediate and lower flowering deciduous plants at the front and sides, choosing plants that fit the growing conditions and that give you pleasure. If the border will be seen in winter, broad-leaved and needled evergreens will add form and interest, and so will the coloured bark and berries of deciduous shrubs (see Chapter 9 and Table 15). The size of the border and the size of the individual plants should be in scale with the size of the yard. If you have a tiny space, you might want to devote it to dwarf evergreens, heaths and heathers, small flowering shrubs, and perhaps a few flowers that merit close viewing.

A more ambitious gardener might choose to combine individual plants in groups of one, three, five or more to form larger patterns. It is usually better to have a few, simple lines to your shrub border, no matter what its size, than to make it busy with too many varieties and groupings. A small border, for example, would look best with a few varieties in a few groupings. Larger borders could have more varieties and a few more groupings, with more and larger plants in each grouping. A good guide is to estimate the kinds and numbers of shrubs and trees you want, then halve the variety and double the number. Planting in drifts helps too, with plants arranged in curves rather than straight lines or clustered in circles.

If you are comfortable with planning at this level, you might want to consider more subtle factors such as form, colour, and texture, described in Chapter 9.

Flowers and shrub borders go together well. The shrubs provide height and form, and the flowers provide seasonal variety in foliage and flowers. It is good to use perennials, annuals (although these are high maintenance plants), spring flowering bulbs, lilies, tender summer bulbs (also high maintenance), and herbs in front of and between shrubs. They fill in gaps in a new shrub border until the shrubs fill out, or you might plan to leave permanent spaces for flowers in your plan. Perhaps you already have a flower border that is too much work or in the wrong place and want to change it over to a shrub border. You could remove a few perennials and plant your shrubs, a few at a time or all in one season, and keep the perennials in place as gap fillers until the shrubs have reached full size. Remember, however, that perennials are often able to win out over young shrubs when competing for moisture and nutrients. Leave plenty of root room for the shrubs. Borders of only flowers are best out of sight in winter, but if you already have one, you could pad it out with a few shrubs to provide winter interest.

Barriers

Most walls of plants that are waist-high or taller are effective on a visual level at keeping out unwelcome visitors. Sometimes, however, a physically unwelcoming barrier is required. The following plants, listed in increasing order of height, are particularly effective at keeping out invaders:

Mahonia	*Yew*
Spanish Gorse	*Sea Buckthorn*
Shrub Roses	*Crabapple*
Japanese Quince	*Russian Olive*
Five-Leaved Aralia	*Hawthorn*
Holly	*Honey-Locust*
Flowering Quince	*Spruce*
Firethorn	

Wild varieties of Crabapple are best and thorny varieties of Shrub Roses, Hawthorn and Honey Locust. The smaller plants can be spaced about 30 cm apart, and the larger ones 70 cm to 100 cm apart and kept heavily sheared. Chicken wire can be woven amongst the plants when young to provide an immediate barrier, and left in place as the plants mature.

Having considered several plants for various functions, you might want to look again at your property, as a whole. Is there a fairly even distribution of evergreens around the lot? Evergreens make good backdrops for deciduous shrubs, but they needn't form a solid wall. Are they concentrated where they will be visible from the house and appreciated in winter? Are the deciduous shrubs fairly well spaced out, and are there enough that they don't look lost and dead among a sea of evergreens? Does their ultimate height match the available growing space? Mark plant positions on your plot plan according to their ultimate height and spread. Are the plants matched to sun and shade and other growing conditions? Many other factors, such as shape, texture and colour, and the theme of the garden, can be taken into account when making the final selection of trees and shrubs, but the basic purpose and growing conditions must be taken care of first.

> Taller plants may be better located on the lower slope of a property to counter-balance the dominant effect of structures and plants on the upper slope.

≈§ Constructed Walls

Sometimes there isn't enough space to plant a living wall, and a constructed wall may be able to serve functions that plants cannot. Constructed walls come in two types: free-standing walls such as fences, trellises, brick or rock walls; and retaining walls such as those used to hold back earth or to shape terraces.

You might recall that walls of various heights serve various functions: knee-high walls give direction and provide seating; waist-high walls direct traffic and partially enclose; head-high walls provide screens and create privacy; and so on. Constructed walls do the same thing, with the added benefit that they may improve drainage and increase the sense of space in a small yard.

Free-standing walls usually take up less space than shrubs of the same height, a decided advantage in small yards. The exception might be dry rock walls, which are almost as wide at the base as they are tall. They might be just the answer, though, if you have a field of rocks in your back yard.

Walls and fences can serve as windbreaks, but care must be taken in building them. If they are solid, they are more expensive, appear dark and imposing, actually create turbulence and are dry at the base. A fence that is 20% open, as many board fences are, or a fence with a baffle at the top, angled at forty-five degrees into the wind, helps to slow down the wind and create shelter without increasing turbulence. Plexiglass can also act as a windbreak, say around a deck, when a view must be preserved. Walls and fences, of course, can also act as screens. Even an open, airy lattice works as a visual barrier.

There are probably height restrictions in the building regulations for your community; it is a good idea to check on these before you build a particularly high wall. If you are building a wall of brick or rock, call in an expert for anything over 1 m high. Fences and trellises can be matched to the house by using similar materials or colours, and many of them can be built by amateurs. Libraries have excellent do-it-yourself manuals for all kinds of projects.

Retaining walls, in conjunction with terraces, open up a world of design possibilities. Terraces are level stretches of ground and may be covered in grass, other plants, paving stones, wood or bricks. They help to break up large spaces and add interest to smooth slopes. In small gardens, adding a terrace and retaining wall can actually help to increase the sense of space. Different heights can be used in building terraces, depending on the slope and the functions to be served, whether for sitting or partial enclosure or privacy. If walls are to be used for sitting, comfortable dimensions are 35 cm to 40 cm high and 40 cm to 45 cm wide.

Retaining walls are of two basic types: solid walls, such as brick or concrete or mortared rock, and porous walls, such as dry rock or wooden or railroad ties. Solid walls are generally more difficult to build, requiring footings and 'dead men' and weep holes. They also tend to look more solid and formal. Porous walls are usually easier to build, though generally they cannot be as tall, and they fit better into an informal setting. Again, for anything over 1 m, it is a good idea to call in an expert.

One big advantage of retaining walls and terraces is that they help control water drainage on steep surfaces by diverting water to the sides instead of straight down. A drainage swale behind the wall helps to do this, so that water does not spill over the top of the wall, particularly in solid walls. If

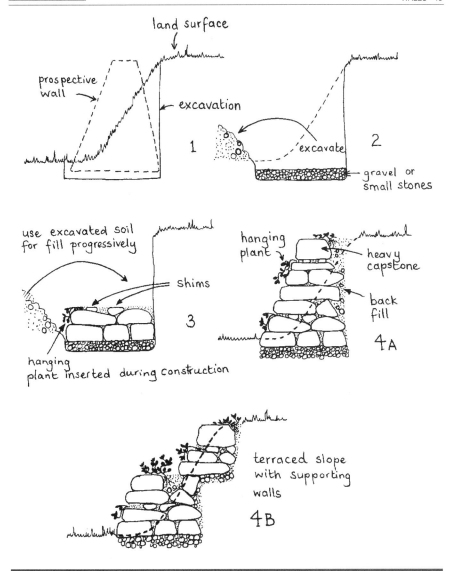

land surface

prospective wall

excavation

1

excavate

2

gravel or small stones

use excavated soil for fill progressively

shims

3

hanging plant inserted during construction

hanging plant

heavy capstone

back fill

4A

terraced slope with supporting walls

4B

The construction of dry stone walls and walled terraces. Dry stone walls must be wider at the base than they are at the top, with the front face sloping back 2 to 3 units for every 12 units rise. 1—Plan the excavation to accommodate the wall. Its position should allow the excavated soil to be used as back fill. 2—Excavate the soil, and provide for drainage with a 15 cm layer of gravel or small stones. 3—Add layers of stones progressively, selecting them with care. Insert wall plants during construction, filling around their roots with enriched garden soil and watering them well. Use small stones (shims) and excavated soil to make up for the unevenness of the stones in each layer. Shims stay in position better if they are placed within the wall rather than at the face, where they may pop out. 4A—The completed wall. Save some of the largest stones for the top of the wall to provide for stability. 4B—A series of terraces is an alternative to a single wall for a high slope. Each wall section is constructed by the methods described above.

porous walls are planted, the plants will benefit from water that seeps through the cracks and crevices.

Whether solid or porous, the size of the individual parts should be in scale with the total size of the wall. Large boulders and bold curves look best on a large property, and small rocks and tight corners are more suited to small spaces. If the wall has to turn corners and follow curves, the individual parts must allow for this; long beams are not very well suited! As well, it helps to tie the landscape together if the materials used match those of the house or deck or are found in surrounding nature.

Constructed walls offer many possibilities not available through the use of plants alone. They may be expensive to build but they offer immediate results. Fences and walls are permanent features, so invest wisely for the long term when you choose the materials and build them.

✌ Combination Walls

Sometimes constructed walls are needed for certain functions but, being in a garden, they cry out to be draped in plants. Combining plants and constructed walls may take the form of growing vines and wall shrubs next to a wall or trellis, training plants in espalier form, using raised planting beds as walls, building berms, or putting plants in a dry rock wall as you build it. Sometimes an unattractive shed or fence or other eyesore benefits from being clothed in plants.

Berms are used in gardens which have access to generous quantities of soil. They are walls of earth, having both functional and design value. They will almost certainly affect surface drainage so their position must be well thought out. Probably the best way to incorporate them into the landscape is to study natural hills and mounds in the area and follow their general shapes. Berms can serve as screens, windbreaks, noise absorbers and as higher patches of land on which to plant. They can also act as additional play surfaces for children, for games in summer and sliding in winter. If you plant them, you can take advantage of the microclimates they offer: warm and sunny on the south and west, and cool and shaded on the north and east. This may allow you to grow plants that you couldn't otherwise. Berms have a lot of versatility, but only if you can find the soil to build them.

There are many design advantages to growing plants on or

against traditional walls. Most importantly, it saves space. Vines growing on a trellis provide excellent screening but take up far less room than a tree or hedge. Fruits and vegetables can be grown in the vertical plane where there is very little space horizontally. Plants growing upwards give height to a design, which helps to create a sense of increased space, even in a very small property or balcony. If a design is flat and horizontal, some vertical elements encourage the eye to travel a greater distance in looking upwards, and this translates into a feeling of greater space.

Plants growing against, on top of, or in a wall also help to soften what might otherwise be an imposing wall. These could be very tall walls, such as rock faces or infill behind wire mesh, or heavy, dark walls such as those made of stone, concrete or brick. When vines such as *Clematis tangutica* or Virginia Creeper grow on top of a wall and hang down, for example, the eye travels downward and the wall seems lower and less imposing.

Plants with a weeping form also draw the eye downwards and are relaxing and restful.

Examples of small weeping trees are, in decreasing order of hardiness:

Weeping Caragana *White or Black Weeping Mulberry*
Young's Weeping Birch *Patterson's Pride Plum*
Weeping Purple Beech *Sargent's Weeping Hemlock*
Red Jade Crabapple *Weeping Japanese Cherry*
  (Cheal's Weeping Cherry)

Trees such as these are usually planted in front of a wall, taking up a fair share of space, but they could also be planted on top of a retaining wall and allowed to trail down. Red Jade Crabapple or Weeping Caragana could be staked and grown to only 1 m high or so, and then allowed to weep generously down a wall. Position such plants 1 m to 2 m away from the wall so that their roots do not disturb the wall.

In smaller gardens, shrubs that tend to be low and trailing and so suited to planting on top of a retaining wall might be more appropriate than weeping trees. Herbaceous plants that drape and trail include *Artemisia, Aubrieta, Cerastium* (Snow-in-Summer), which spreads rather too generously at times, *Campanula, Dianthus, Phlox subulata* (Moss Pink) and various creeping *Thymus*.

Plants that have a spreading form are also highly recommended for planting in front of walls. Many of the plants listed in Table 3 have this form and make excellent wall plants.

One result of growing shrubs against walls is that they often grow taller than when are freestanding. Pyracantha, for example, does well to reach 2 m growing in the open, but sometimes reaches nearly 3 m against a sheltered wall.

If roses are planted against a wall, there is a choice between low, spreading kinds (such as Nitida Defender, red or white *Rugosa repens*, Red Max Graf, Swany and Sea Foam), and upright varieties that can be tied in place and used as climbers (such as Henry Kelsey, John Cabot, Polestar and William Baffin). True climbing roses can also be used, but they need

Dry stone walls can be very attractive, particularly when the inserted plants become established. A wide variety of plants are suited to the dry conditions of a stone wall. Weeping and draping plant forms are particularly attractive and include herbaceous perennials such as *Antennaria, Anthemis, Arabis, Arenaria, Artemisia, Aubrieta, Aurinia, Campanula, Dianthus, Dicentra eximia, Draba, Euphorbia, Gypsophila, Helianthemum, Heuchera, Hypericum, Iberis, Penstemon, Phlox, Potentilla, Sedum, Sempervivum, Silene, Thymus, Tiarella* and *Veronica*. Additional plants, suited to growing in front of walls or on the top, are listed in Table 3.

the extra attention of taking down and mulching each fall, because most of them are too tender to survive harsh winters very well.

Trailing Junipers that can be used on top of walls include varieties such as Blue Pacific and Waukegan. Low, spreading varieties that could be used on top of walls or at the foot include Arcadia and Blue Danube. Larger varieties with a tendency to horizontal spreading, ideal for the foot of a large wall, include Gold Coast, Sea Green and Pfitzer. Nurseries vary in the kinds of Junipers they carry, so look at the shapes carefully and choose the ones you want from the varieties available. Microbiota, discovered in Siberia, is a low-growing, near ally of Junipers. It has a lacey, feathery look to it but is remarkably hardy and tolerant of poor growing conditions. There are also some attractive spreading Yews available although they tend to be rather large dark plants. Some of the False Cypresses have a very lacy spreading shape, ideal for lightening a heavy, dark wall. An example of these would be Golden Threadleaf False Cypress.

To get the most out of wall plants, it helps to know how they grow and suitable methods of attachment. Some vines grow by twining their stems, leaves or tendrils and can climb up netting, a trellis, wire mesh, a chain-link fence, into a tree, or any free-standing structure around which they can wrap. Other vines climb by clinging holdfasts or disks and can attach themselves directly to stone walls, rough bark, brick work or any other surface. They have the distinct disadvantage, though, of increasing the deterioration of the surface on which they grow. This is especially difficult if they grow against a wooden house which needs periodic painting and repair.

One way to have the best of both worlds is to grow vines on trellises that can be laid on the ground, vine and all, when the wall needs maintenance. This has two other advantages for the vines themselves. Planting them out from the wall 50 cm or more, with their roots directed away from the wall, gets them away from the driest soil right next to the wall; and growing them some distance from the wall allows better air circulation, which reduces disease. Many vines make good backdrops for flowers, and several kinds of vines can be grown together. You might want to combine foliage and flowering vines, or two kinds of flowering climbers, such as blue Clematis and pink Roses. If Clematis vines are grown through shrubs or trees, choose varieties that are cut back each spring.

If you grow wall shrubs you may or may not want to attach them. Many of them can be left to grow freely, their main attraction being that they have a spreading form suitable to wall growing. If you want to restrain them slightly, you could very loosely and gently attach some of the branches to the wall. When tying shrubs or vines in place, it is best to use soft fabric or leather straps. Old socks and pantyhose are ideal, but metal is about the worst thing to use because it overheats and cuts into the plants.

The extreme form of tying trees and shrubs to walls is known as espalier. This involves training the branches into special patterns that hold the plant against a wall. It is an excellent method for saving space and has been used for hundreds of years in Europe. Its use is beginning to catch on in North America in small gardens where gardeners are trying new ideas.

When espalier is mentioned, the picture that usually comes to mind is fruit trees trained against a wall. In fact, any shrubs suitable for growing against walls can be trained in formal espalier patterns. The size of a tree or a shrub is often smaller than when grown in the open because the branches are directed sideways or diagonally and the growth is carefully

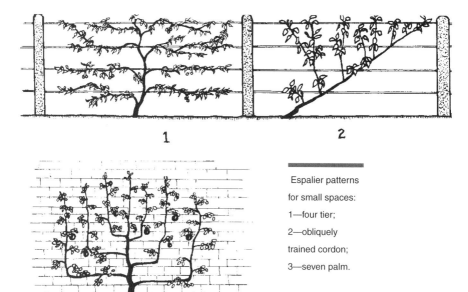

1

2

3

Espalier patterns
for small spaces:
1—four tier;
2—obliquely
trained cordon;
3—seven palm.

controlled. More informal espaliers can be grown, with less restriction to growth and patterned according to your whim.

The espalier technique need not be used against a wall at all. If you like the idea of growing trees and shrubs in a flat plane to reduce space or to create interest, you can grow them on wires stretched between two posts. The plants themselves then form the wall. Chain-link fence can also be covered in espaliered plants.

Free-standing walls can be built as raised beds for shrubs or flowers. This makes gardening easier and provides ready opportunity for people to enjoy the scent, colour and touch of plants.

If you are interested in growing plants directly on a retaining or free-standing wall, or if you want to soften a rock face, you might want to investigate rockery plants. Many of these perennials are suitable for planting directly in walls and in cracks and crevices:

Arabis (Rock Cress)	*Penstemon*
Arenaria	*Phlox (Moss Pink)*
Armeria (Thrift)	*Poppies*
Aubrieta	*Potentilla*
Campanula	*Saxifrage*
Dianthus (Pinks)	*Sedum*
Draba	*Sempervivum*
Heuchera	*Thyme*
Lychnis	*Veronica*

A few shrubs that are suitable for such a situation include Rock Rose *(Helianthemum)*, St. John's Wort, Evergreen Candytuft *(Iberis)*, and Garland Flower (Rose Daphne). Both herbaceous perennials and shrubs are best planted in the wall as it is being constructed.

If you do grow shrubs or vines against walls, especially solid walls, there are two problems you might encounter: dryness and extremes of heat and cold. Knowing that solid walls can be very dry at the base, you will probably want to work into the soil lots of organic matter to help retain moisture. A generous layer of mulch will also help. Dryness does not seem to be so much a problem beside more open walls such as fences and trellises. Extremes of heat and cold are encountered on south and north facing walls. Walls with a southern exposure reflect back the heat of a summer sun, which can be very hard on some plants. They will also tend to heat up earlier in the spring, perhaps fooling plants into thinking that spring has arrived. This often leads to tender buds being nipped by frost.

Plants growing against a north-facing wall will receive very little light and must be carefully selected for shade tolerance. They will also be late to start growth in spring because of extended coolness. These need not be disadvantages, however, if the plant material is selected to suit the conditions. An east-facing wall, for example, may be ideal for plants that like a cool situation, and a west-facing wall may provide the warmth and protection needed for heat-loving plants. A wall with a southern exposure might get protection from excessive midday heat by an overhang, as against a garage wall, for example. Care must be taken that the overhang isn't too wide and doesn't produce too much shade. Overhangs also contribute to dryness.

☙ Pruning and Rejuvenation

Whenever living material is used for walls, or in conjunction with inanimate walls, it must be in good condition to look its best. Employing good pruning practices from when the plant is very young will help ensure this. Sometimes a planting can get out of hand, with overgrown shrubs needing rejuvenation.

Most deciduous shrubs and a good many evergreens can be rejuvenated, but how it is done varies with the type of plant material. Sometimes, too, a plant is nearing the end of its natural lifespan and no amount of restorative pruning will help. Daphne, for example, does well if it lasts for 15 years, so it doesn't make sense to try to restore a 12-year-old plant.

Needled Evergreens

Needled evergreens make most of their annual growth in the first few weeks of spring. One or two light shearings is all that is needed to restrict their growth or make them grow dense. In a windbreak, for example, you might want to shear the tops and sides while the trees are very young to make them grow tight and close to the ground. You might do the same for evergreen hedges, remembering to start while the plants are young, and keeping them in the shape you want right from the beginning. It is no good to simply lop off the top of an evergreen hedge without trimming the sides as well because the hedge will lose its natural shape which is well designed for shedding snow and preventing breakage.

To shear an evergreen, cut off about one-third of the new growth on the tips of the branches soon after growth starts in spring. On evergreens with an all-over pattern of growth, such as Cedars *(Thuja)* and Junipers, hedge clippers are often used to give an all-over light shearing. These plants can be shortened by as much as one-third and reshaped on the sides if a rejuvenation is required. They may look a little shorn for a few years, but the scars will eventually grow over. Yews, too, can have as much as one-third of their green material removed for drastic restoration, or even cut back to within a few centimetres of the ground if absolutely necessary. It will take several years, however, before they start to look at all good again.

On other evergreens that grow in whorls, such as Spruce, Fir, Pine and Hemlock, individual branch tips are cut back, usually with a pair of secateurs. On Spruce the new growth is quite short; on Pines the long candles should be cut back by one half when almost fully extended but still closed. Whorled plants cannot be severely cut back to rejuvenate them; if this is done, they will always look as though they had been beheaded and will never regain their natural shape.

Coniferous evergreens with an all-over pattern of growth (left) or whorled pattern (right) require different methods of pruning, as explained in the text.

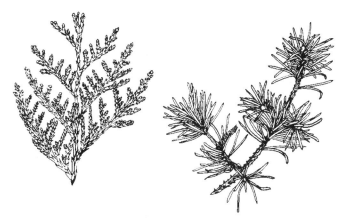

After spring growth is well established on evergreens, the centre tip of side branches can be cut out completely to give denser growth. Low-growing Junipers can be cut back to a strong side shoot, or the leaders can be cut out completely. Don't do this to tall evergreens unless you want them short and dense for hedges, because even a light pruning of the central growing point causes the main stem to fork.

Gardeners sometimes hesitate to shear evergreens, thinking that they will do it when the plant reaches the desired height. In every case, it is better to start shearing when the plant is young. A light shearing each spring can continue indefinitely, or it can be stopped once the plant gets too tall, or when it has attained the desired shape. The most important thing is to understand why it is being done in the first place.

Of course, there is no law that says evergreens must be sheared. It is done only to restrict growth and to create a denser plant. Pruning for the health of the plant, however, should always be carried out, and entire branches can be cut out if they are dead, diseased or broken. This sort of pruning is best done as soon as the need is noticed.

To help prevent breakage, remove heavy snow loads in winter by lifting branches upwards. If the tip of a spruce or similar tree is accidently broken off, a new leader can be trained. If the damage is less than a year old, clipping back all but the most central of the competing leaders will help to establish a new central leader. On trees less recently damaged, a young supple side branch can be tied in place in an upright position and trained as a new leader.

Broad-leaved Evergreens

Broad-leaved evergreens, such as Rhododendrons, Mountain Laurel and some Azaleas, are pruned in a manner entirely different from that for needled evergreens. Most of the annual pruning, if any is needed at all, would be pinching back the new growth one to three times during the growing season. Snipping off the terminal leaves like this encourages the latent laterals to grow, giving a denser shrub, and should be completed by mid-July.

Some broad-leaved evergreens, such as Box and Holly, can be clipped during the growing season if they are being grown as hedges. Box and Holly usually grow slowly, so a single annual clipping in the spring is usually all that is required.

Drastic pruning can be done during dormancy in early spring to remove dead, diseased or broken branches. Broad-leaved evergreens can be severely damaged by winter winds if they are not well watered and mulched each autumn. It is unwise, though, to be hasty in spring in cutting out what appear to be winter-killed branches. These evergreens can make surprising recoveries, and it is best to delay branch removal until new growth starts, when true winter-kill can be clearly identified. Leaves drop off naturally after two or three years of life anyway, so it is best to let the branches carry on growing naturally if the tips are still alive.

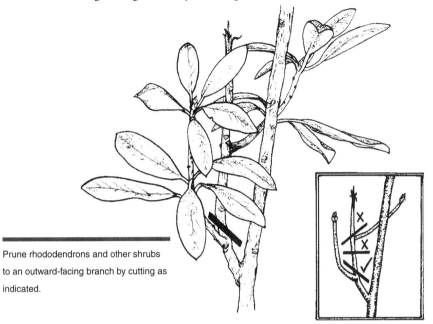

Prune rhododendrons and other shrubs to an outward-facing branch by cutting as indicated.

If some branches have grown too long, they can be shortened after spring bloom by cutting back to an outward-facing branch. Holly pruning can be delayed until late autumn, in time for cutting Christmas decorations. It is best to prune on a mild day because freezing temperatures can cause cracks in the bark during the pruning process.

If pruning is done along these lines, little rejuvenation should be required. If it is necessary, it is best carried out over two or three years by removing a few of the oldest branches close to the ground each spring during dormancy. In this way, there is less shock to the plant and less of a gap in the shrub and landscape. Pieris and Mahonia can have all their main branches cut back severely in the spring, but this is rarely required and is a rather drastic measure. Box and Holly hedges can be cut back quite severely, but they are so slow growing that rejuvenation is not usually a problem with them. If it has to be done, it is best to remove no more than one-third of the green material during dormancy in early spring.

As a general rule use a cautious hand in pruning evergreens, which also means less time spent pruning than that required for faster growing deciduous material.

Deciduous Plants

Unlike needled evergreens, deciduous plants grow throughout the warm season and are usually pruned at one of two times during the year. Plants that bloom in the summer on new growth are pruned during dormancy before they bloom, and plants that bloom in the spring on last season's growth are pruned immediately after flowering. In this way flower buds are not cut away and flowering is not reduced.

Hydrangeas can be confusing; those with flowers in dense balls or cones are pruned while dormant (Hills-of-Snow, Annabelle, PeeGee), whereas the Lacecaps and those with flowers in loose balls or cones (Bigleaf, Oakleaf) are pruned after blooming, if at all.

Shrubs grown for their coloured stems, such as Kerria, Dogwood and Flowering Raspberry, are pruned in spring to encourage the growth of young, more brightly coloured stems.

The timing of pruning might be a consideration for shrub selection for various situations. At a cottage, for example, you might prefer to plant shrubs that bloom early in the season when you first go there and that need pruning after flowering when you have more time. In a city garden, where you are more likely to have time during the dormant season to do the required pruning, you might want to focus on summer flowering shrubs.

Most climbers and vines need little pruning, unless they become overgrown tangles. Dense growth is best thinned early in the spring, when it is easier to follow the course of the stems. Clematis is pruned back hard or only lightly, depending on variety, but always in early spring. Early varieties that bloom in late spring on old wood, with perhaps a repeat bloom in late summer on new wood, are pruned back only lightly until live wood is reached. These include Bee's Jubilee, Duchess of Edinburgh, Miss Bateman, Nelly Moser, The President and Vyvyan Pennell. More commonly grown are the late varieties of Clematis that bloom on new wood, such as Comtesse de Bouchard, Ernest Markham, Gypsy Queen, Hagley Hybrid, Huldine, Jackmanii, Lady Betty Balfour, Perle d'Azur and Ville de Lyon. These can be pruned back hard to 50 cm or 100 cm in spring and are a better choice for harsher zones. Some Clematis can be pruned lightly or hard, depending on whether early or late flowering is desired. Elsa Spaeth, Henryi, Ramona, Silver Moon and William Kennett will produce large flowers on old wood in spring if they are pruned lightly, but will bloom vigorously on new wood from midsummer on if pruned hard in spring.

Wisteria is exceptional in needing regular summer pruning. In fact, if your Wisteria won't bloom, prune back side shoots three times during the growing season, keep it on the dry side if you can, withhold nitrogen, and try root pruning if all else fails.

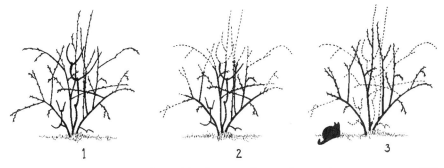

1—A crowded, overgrown shrub.
2— Pruned incorrectly, the shrub has been given a "haircut."
3—Pruned correctly, dead, damaged and diseased wood has been removed. Crossed and rubbing branches are also removed. Old growth is cut off close to the ground.

An informal hedge usually needs pruning once a year. If it is a flowering hedge, the timing would be in accordance with the pattern set out above. An informal hedge that is grown mainly for its foliage can be pruned during dormancy or after the first flush of spring growth. For informal hedges, or for individual shrubs, pruning is done to help shape the plant and to keep it within bounds. Older wood is removed regularly to encourage young growth and to keep the shrub from becoming too dense. It is best not to shear shrubs in this situation because giving them a haircut detracts from their natural shape and tends to reduce blooming. It is quite all right, however, to tip the occasional branch that has grown too long.

Formally clipped hedges may require pruning as many as three times during the year: early in the spring during dormancy; after the initial spring burst of growth; and towards the middle or end of July. A slow-growing formal hedge might require pruning only once a year, usually after the spring burst. For formal hedges, light all-over shearing helps to keep the hedge dense and within bounds and in the best shape for hedges (top narrower than the base).

For any shrub or hedge, the dead, diseased and broken branches can be removed at any time, always cutting back to an outward-facing branch or bud.

If deciduous shrubs have not been regularly pruned or have simply grown old and overcrowded, they can often be rejuvenated quite readily.

Formal hedges are often cut back drastically, with good results, but they are usually fast growing, vigorous shrubs. The same can be done for individual shrubs, but it is rather a shock to the plants, and it does leave a gap in the landscape.

A better method, both for informal hedges and individual shrubs, is to spread the process over three years. This is done by cutting out at the base one-third of the oldest branches each year for three years. This allows the shrub or hedge to maintain its function in the landscape, reduces shock to the plant and encourages young growth from the base. It is usually done with Cotoneaster, Hibiscus, Mock Orange, Honeysuckle shrubs, Viburnums and Lilacs. This type of rejuvenation pruning is usually best done in early spring during dormancy, although it can be left until after blooming for spring flowering shrubs. For Lilacs, in fact, it is sometimes recommended to wait until after flowering to reduce the amount of suckers that arise.

Methods of pruning and rejuvenation for particular plants can vary, and for detailed descriptions of methods it might be wise to consult some of the many pruning books available at public libraries.

CHAPTER 4

Floors

nce the ceilings and walls of your design are in place, the floor can be considered. You might choose inert substances such as gravel and shredded bark, constructed surfaces such as patios and decks, or living groundcovers such as lawns and low shrubs.

Functionally, floors can bring warmth or coolness to your outdoor living areas, smother weeds, control erosion and fill in awkward shapes and spaces in your plant cover. As design features they can direct traffic, create interest, change the sense of space and unify the various outdoor rooms.

⇜ Constructed and Inert Floors
The practicality of constructed floors and floors of inert materials can be weighed into the design of your garden, both for looks and for maintenance. They can be planned to be much less demanding of maintenance time than, say, a lawn or a bed of living groundcover. They can make an outdoor room warmer or cooler and also can make a statement about the style of the garden.

Wood, for example, looks and feels warmer than stone, and dark-coloured stone absorbs heat better than light-coloured concrete. Brick looks more formal than wood, and uniform, regular paving stones look more formal than crazy paving.

A flagstone path is an ideal setting for low, creeping plants that are resistant to being walked on. Try Arabis, Arenaria, Artemisia, Chamomile, Dianthus, Draba, Mazus, Thymus, and Veronica.

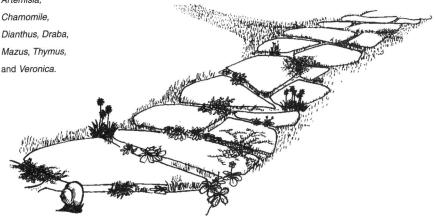

Wooden decks can be styled formally or informally, and patio surfaces can be made of concrete or brick or stone.

Materials we usually think of as mulches for weed suppression or erosion control can also be thought of as flooring materials and can give considerable variety to the feel of a garden. Gravel is often used in contemporary style landscapes, shredded bark or pine needles or pine cones are more informal, and bark chips could be used for either situation. Lava rock is sometimes used, but it looks too harsh for most gardens. Whatever you use should be consistent with the style and proportions of your house and garden.

It is also worth considering how much erosion control is necessary. Porous flooring materials are better for drainage and erosion control. In a patio or path, for example, stones or brick set into a bed of sand can absorb and control run-off better than the same materials set in concrete, and mulches of gravel are less likely to be washed away than bark nuggets. Porous materials are also healthier for plants especially where shallow-rooted trees and shrubs have their roots covered. Shredded bark is perhaps the most attractive, natural-looking mulch available. It is much finer than bark nuggets, stays in place on slopes, and does a superb job of weed suppression.

It is a good idea to be consistent in the choice of materials throughout so that your garden has some unity. For example, you might want to use shredded bark as a mulch in your shrub border and as a covering for informal paths; alternatively,

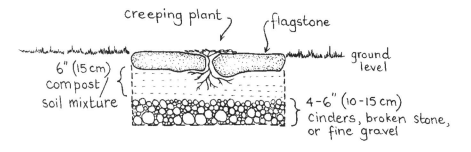

Construction of a flagstone path. Dig a 30 cm deep trench. Place a layer of gravel in the bottom of the trench, and then a soil mixture that both holds moisture and drains well. Level the soil and lightly firm it. The trench must be filled to the top before the flagstones are added because the level will drop after the flagstones have been added and the soil has settled. Press the flagstones into position, and water well to settle the flagstones and soil.

evenly-sized gravel suits a formal setting near the house and driveway, and rocks of unequal size are better in an informal setting further away. Where stone has been used to build a garden wall, it will be complemented in a patio or garden steps, and brick fits in well if you have brick on your house.

Decks

A deck or patio is a versatile feature in your landscape and an almost universal feature in new housing. When the lawn is still wet and even frozen, a constructed floor provides a place to situate oneself in comfort. One that is attached to your house is a room that creates a transition between the interior of the house and the natural setting of the garden.

A deck can be built at ground level or elevated, perhaps to provide a view over the treetops. An upper story deck also increases the amount of floor area of your lot, creating another kind of space underneath it. This might be storage space or gardening space for appropriate shrubs or groundcover.

One situation that may prove difficult is determining patio or deck size. Some ideas that might help you keep your deck in scale with the rest of its surroundings and the right size for your family is as follows. For an average size, you can allow 4 square metres per family member, up to 6 square metres for a large house and yard, and down to 2 square metres per person for a small house and yard. If you do a lot of entertaining outdoors in the summer, build bigger; if you want a more intimate area, build smaller. Another guideline is to make it approximately the same size as an adjoining room in the house. Thus, an intimate patio or sideyard adjoining a bedroom would be much smaller than a family patio adjoining a living room. As to minimum size, the only stipulation is that it should be at least 2 m wide; if it is narrower, it is very unlikely that anyone will use it.

Living Floors

Plants used to cover garden floors function in several ways. They help control weeds, reduce erosion, conserve moisture, modify outdoor temperatures, direct traffic and give unity to a garden. They come in many forms, as annuals, perennials, grasses, ferns, and deciduous and evergreen shrubs. Choosing the right plants depends on the growing conditions you have and on knowing what you want them to accomplish.

Erosion control is an important function of groundcovers on slopes. The leaves slow down the rate at which water reaches the ground, and the network of roots creates a porous soil which acts as a sponge. While groundcovers are reducing erosion, they are also acting as mulches by suppressing weed growth and conserving moisture, and they bring beauty to the landscape as well.

Plants used as groundcovers can have a cooling effect where heat build-up is a problem: on a south-facing area, a covering of grass or other greenery can be considerably cooler than one of brick. If you live in a chilly coastal location, however, you might well opt for the warmer brick.

A variety of plants are suitable as ground covers, including some annuals such as nasturtium. The taller ones, such as juniper, require less maintenance as they are better at smothering weeds than low plants. Evergreens provide interest in winter. There are shade tolerant plants to choose from, such as ferns, and plants

Plants can also be used to direct traffic. Visitors to your garden would think nothing of walking on grass, but a groundcover of ferns or shrubs discourages foot traffic. You can have a lot of fun planning routes with plants, choosing Thrift or Creeping Thyme where there is light traffic, Chamomile or Veronica where there is slightly heavier traffic, and rugged lawn grasses for heavy-duty use.

that fill the senses, such as roses with their fragrant flowers and colourful hips.

Groundcover plants can create unity in a garden. Lawns that sweep from one end of the garden to the other help to tie together every outdoor room into a whole. If you dislike mowing, or are tired of grass, or simply want something different, you might want to try such ground covers as Baltic Ivy, Crown Vetch or Japanese Spurge (none of which is suitable for foot traffic).

Unity can be accomplished with other groundcovers as well, though with slightly more thought and effort. The same groundcover can be used under shrubs throughout the garden, or along the driveway, and by garden paths. It is subtle but effective clues such as this that help tie together the separate parts of a garden. As much as possible, use flooring materials and plants with little or no interruption, keeping the cover continuous.

Vines and shrubs work well as groundcovers and tend to be more permanent than perennials. Table 6 lists both herbaceous perennials and woody plants that serve well as groundcovers for smothering weeds, and some of them double as covers for slopes to reduce or prevent erosion. Others are better suited as lawn substitutes or as touches of colour in an unexpected place. Some can tolerate steady or occasional foot traffic. All of them grow well in moist, well-drained sites, but several can tolerate dry conditions.

Many of the perennial groundcovers are effective as underplantings for spring flowering bulbs. Arenaria, Sweet Woodruff, Campanula, Aubrieta and Mint, as well as Iberis, *Vinca minor* and Creeping Thyme are also effective, but Daylilies should be avoided. In all cases, the height of the groundcover should be half the height of the bulb flower stem. It also looks more attractive if the bulb flower contrasts with the groundcover flower; coloured Tulips rather than white ones with white Iberis, for example.

Some roses that work well as groundcovers are Nitida Defender, *Rugosa repens alba* and *rosea*, Dart's Dash, Henry Hudson, Moje Hammarberg, Sea Foam, Charles Albanel, Red Max Graf, and Swany.

Less well know herbaceous plants can also be used as groundcovers in small areas, including Alchemilla, Aubrieta, Foamflower (Tiarella), Helleborus, Saxifrage and Sweet Woodruff. Cliff Green (Pachystima) is a little known, fine-textured evergreen plant that goes very well as a groundcover under Rhododendrons. Ferns, too, especially evergreen species where they can be seen in winter, make very attractive groundcovers.

If you have a rented garden or will be residing only a short time in your present home, you might want to use annuals as groundcovers. Although they are effective only during the growing season, they are considerably cheaper than perennials and shrubs. Low, spreading kinds seem to be best, such as Ageratum (Flossflower), Sweet Alyssum, Nasturtiums, Impatiens, Pansies, Portulaca and Petunias, particularly the trailing varieties. If you plant perennials or woody plants as groundcovers, you could use annuals the first year to help fill in the spaces until the permanent cover closes over. It also helps reduce the number of permanent plants you must purchase if you can fill in the gaps with annuals for a while.

In trying to decide between lawns and other groundcover plants, it is generally wiser to use groundcovers if one or more of the following conditions exist: less than 6 hours of sun each day; a slope greater than one unit rise for each three units horizontal; very dry conditions; small areas too awkward for mowing; or areas disconnected from other lawn areas.

Ground covers as a substitute for grass in shady areas include *Hosta* (above), *Vinca minor* (periwinkle), *Pachysandra* (Japanese Spurge), *Dicentra eximia* (fringed bleeding heart), *Ajuga* (bugleweed), *Pulmonaria* (William and Mary), and *Polygonatum* (Solomon's seal).

Spacing and Arranging

How closely you space plants depends on their ultimate size, their rate of growth, slope of the ground and the expense. For example, low growing plants such as Sedum, Dianthus, Thrift, Chamomile, Japanese Spurge, Ajuga and Creeping Thyme can be planted 15 cm to 30 cm apart. Larger plants, such as Lamb's Ear, Bearberry, *Phlox subulata* (Moss Pink) and Iberis, can be planted 30 cm to 45 cm apart. Small shrubs, such as shrub roses, Anthony Waterer Spirea, Cinquefoil (Potentilla), Japanese Quince and spreading Junipers, can be planted 60 cm to 120 cm apart. Vines, with their sprawling habit of growth, can be planted 1 m to 2 m apart.

If you have slow-growing plants, or if you want plants to fill in rapidly, use a closer spacing. On a slope, where erosion is a potential problem until the plants fill in, they should also be planted closer. Virginia Creeper, for example, would be planted 2 m apart on the flat but 1 m apart on a slope.

One way to provide enough material for dense planting is to propagate at home, instead of purchasing. The aim is to eventually have a solid layer of vegetation, with no breaks in it for opportunistic weeds and loss of moisture.

When putting plants in the ground, a staggered row system seems to work best. Plants are usually planted one of a kind in a mass, but there is no reason not to mix groundcover plants. Contrasts in texture, a mix of evergreen and deciduous and different times of blooming are some of the ways of introducing variety. Just be sure to use large drifts of each kind so that the effect is not spotty.

✑ Scale

Whether you use inert materials or plants as flooring in the garden, scale is perhaps the most important factor in using them effectively. The size of the yard, the size of the area to be covered, and the unit size of the material or plant, must be congruent. For example, a large yard needs a large deck; a small space needs low-growing, small-leaved plants; small gravel looks better close to a small house, working towards larger gravel and rocks further away; large, coarse-textured plants fit large areas more appropriately some distance away; and so on. Generally speaking, the perennial plants listed in Table 6 are small and low growing and look better in small spaces, whereas the shrubs listed are more appropriate for larger areas. You could, of course, use a shrub in a small space as an accent plant. There are no hard and fast rules, just general guidelines and common sense. It is really quite easy to take scale into account when planning the floors in your garden.

✑ Maintenance

After considering the functions of the floors and, where necessary, the growing conditions, you will need to consider maintenance before making a final decision on what materials or plants to use. The greatest glutton of your time will almost certainly be the lawn, and even supposedly care-free groundcovers will require an initially large investment in time for preparing the soil, planting and weeding. Even inert materials require maintenance time. Gravel mulches should be raked and kept clear of debris, and bark mulches must be renewed by adding a fresh layer about every three years. Wood requires more upkeep than stone. No matter what you choose, though, there are probably ways to cut down on maintenance.

If you take a long-term look at your situation, you might opt to make the effort now of replacing stretches of your lawn with other groundcovers. It is easier when younger to do heavy work in the garden, aiming all the time to reduce the time spent mowing and weeding in later years. Or you might decide, conversely, that you will save some of the more time-consuming gardening for retirement years.

If you plant perennials as groundcovers, you can cut down considerably on maintenance by completely stripping the ground of all weeds and other vegetation before planting. Better yet, work them into the deeper layers of soil so that they are buried under a minimum of 20 cm of topsoil. Another useful technique to reduce weeds and grass on the newly turned ground is to plant a cover crop the first year (see Chapter 6 under Soil Preparation). Even with careful preparation, be vigilant in weeding the first two years after the groundcover is planted. Applying a 6 cm to 8 cm mulch after the ground warms up in spring will also help to reduce weed growth.

If you want to contain rampant growers, a 15 cm wide strip of metal or plastic pushed into the ground will act as a barrier, saving endless hours of pulling out unwanted plants. This is especially important for such plants as Speedwell, Snow-in-Summer and Ajuga (Bugleweed). Rampant vines, such as Bittersweet, Crown Vetch, Honeysuckle, Virginia Creeper and Five-Leaf Akebia, should also be contained, or grown in areas where they can spread freely. An annual shearing is beneficial in containing rampant vines. Some plants are so invasive that they should never be used as groundcovers. Two notorious ones are Goutweed (Bishop's Weed) and Japanese Knotweed.

Some plants benefit from a light shearing each year, usually after flowering. These include Iberis, Lavender, Dianthus, Snow-in-Summer and Heather. Chamomile can even be mowed.

Lawn areas that are simply shaped, with no sharp corners, no island plantings and with a good mowing strip in place, will shave hours off mowing time in just one summer. If you particularly want to have island plantings, make beds three times as long as they are wide and locate them near the edge rather than the middle of the yard.

A mowing strip can be made of wood or brick or any other material that you have used in other areas of your garden.

The wheels of your mower must ride on a level surface that also goes deep enough into the ground to keep the grass from creeping out of bounds. Use mowing strips to edge flower beds, shrub borders, garden paths or any other area where grass meets non-grass. Again, this requires a large investment in time initially that will save huge amounts over the years. Lawn trimmers are useful, or you can cheerfully accept ragged edges to your lawn.

Correct timing of fertilizer application can also save you mowing time. The best times to fertilize are in early spring and in autumn. Applying fertilizer in the summer will only necessitate more frequent mowing at a time when there are a thousand and one other jobs needing attention in the garden. If there is a good mix of clover in your lawn, there is less need to use fertilizer. Grass clippings should also be allowed to decompose in place, unless they are so thick that they smother the lawn.

Ferns are a fairly low-maintenance plant as long as they have light to moderate shade, moisture, and a slightly acidic soil. There are a few ferns which spread pervasively and are best avoided unless you have a large wild area you want filled in. These include Hay-Scented Fern, Lady Fern, Bracken and Sensitive Fern (see also pages 90-91).

Maintenance might be the least of your concerns when you are planning a garden, but it is a major consideration in the years that follow.

If you know you have the right plants, then turn your attention to rejuvenating them.

✌️ Rejuvenation

Perhaps the floors in your garden are fine in position and content but are looking ragged around the edges, or weedy or rotten in the middle. It is usually a fairly straightforward decision to repair a sagging deck or replace unsafe steps, but deciding what to do with the weed-infested lawn or failing groundcover is not so easy.

The first step is to make sure that the right plants are growing in a particular situation. The sun-loving perennials that were planted several years ago may now in fact be shaded out by maturing trees. Children might be using a yard that just cannot tolerate foot traffic. Maybe the lawn grasses were chosen for sun and beauty, and are now subjected to recreational activities and competition with trees.

If you know you have the right plants, then turn your

attention to rejuvenating them. Shrub renewal follows the method outlined in Chapter 3, and herbaceous perennials will certainly benefit from weeding, a topdressing of rotted manure or compost, and removal or division of older plants.

Lawn rejuvenation, however, is usually a bigger proposition because of the larger areas involved, but it is not particularly difficult. If your lawn has 50% or more of desirable grasses and less than 50% weeds, it can be rejuvenated without ripping it up and starting over. If, however, there is less than 15 cm of good topsoil, it is better to start over. Everything you do in the rejuvenating process will be aimed at improving the growing conditions of the lawn grasses so that they can outcompete the weeds and undesirable grasses. The steps are as follows:

1 • If compaction is a problem (grass roots penetrate less than 10 cm into the soil, water is slow to drain), rent a spiking or coring machine to aerate your lawn. Use a special, hollow-tine aerating fork instead if you have a small lawn. This will also help to improve drainage.

2 • Spread garden lime if the pH is less than 6.5, using a rate of 36 kg per 100 sq m of lawn. Two weeks later, or after a heavy rain, spread an organic lawn fertilizer. If you prefer, you can plant your lawn to one-fifth clover to supply the necessary nitrogen. This was common practice in the days before commercial fertilizers.

3 • Dig out deep-rooted weeds in the spring when their food reserves are lowest, and fill in any resulting bare spots with a bit of grass seed. Dandelions are an indication of low nutrient levels and soil compaction. If you insist on using weed killer, one application in late spring is sufficient, but with regular lawn care there is no need to use herbicides.

4 • Mow your lawn regularly and consistently—once a week in spring and fall and during dry spells, and twice a week throughout summer. Regular mowing is essential so that no more than one-third of the height of the grass is removed at one time, thereby reducing shock to the plants. For most lawns a height of 6 cm to 8 cm is recommended; if it is too tall, coarse grasses will take over, and if it is too low, weeds

Following these steps will bring a marked improvement to a run down lawn in just one year, and is far less work and expense than replanting an entire lawn.

will take over. Mow at right angles to the direction in which you last mowed. Leave the grass clippings in place, unless they are longer than 2.5 cm, or use a mulch mower.

5 • Water deeply during dry spells. This means supplying a minimum of 3 cm of water once a week, not a light sprinkling every day. Roots are generally as deep as the grass is tall, so you might want to set your mower higher if you are concerned about dry spells.

In autumn, the following steps can be carried out:

1 • If the thatch is more than 6 mm thick, vigorously rake the lawn and compost the duff. Alternatively, rent a dethatching machine or hire a lawn care company to dethatch.

2 • Measure the pH, and spread lime again if the pH is less than 6.5. Repeat every six months until the desired level is reached. Thereafter, liming should be required only once every 3 or 4 years, unless synthetic fertilizers are used.

3 • To add organic matter to the soil, apply an organic top dressing of good soil plus sand plus shredded compost. Apply at the rate of one bucketful to every three or four square metres, and brush or rake it in with the back of a rake so that the grasses are not buried. This helps to fill in low spots.

4 • Carry out lawn repairs by levelling bumps, filling depressions, and reseeding bare or brown patches. This could be done in spring, if preferred.

Following these steps will bring a marked improvement to a run down lawn in just one year, and is far less work and expense than replanting an entire lawn. It also means that there is no need to hire lawn "experts" to take care of your lawn. All lawn care is within the capabilities of the average home gardener.

If moss is a problem, it is usually an indication of one or more of the following conditions: less than six hours of sun each day, poor drainage, low soil fertility and soil that is too acidic for grasses. If you remedy the problems by proper cultural techniques, you will not have to buy moss killer. Lime and fertilize your lawn, aerate the soil to improve drainage, scratch out the moss, and fill in the gaps with lawn seed. If shade is the problem, you can try the ploys discussed under Light in Chapter 6, or shrug your shoulders and develop an appreciation for soft, velvety moss lawns. They really do look luxurious provided there is little foot traffic.

If you end up deciding that a new lawn is the answer, seed in the spring before the lilacs bloom. Fall planting is better, however, so that grass roots can be well established before they have to tolerate the stresses of summer drought. As soon as evenings start to cool in late summer, plant the seed. Depending on the weather, lawns can be seeded as late as four weeks before the first expected frost date. If you prefer faster results and can afford the extra cost, or if you are planting on a slope, use sods instead of seed. Depending on the weather, these can be laid as late as four to six weeks before the ground usually freezes solid. Sod quality is variable, so buy in one lot from a reputable dealer. Lawns can also be started in spring, especially those containing perennial ryegrass, but try to start early while the weather is still cool and before the lilacs bloom. No matter when you seed, regular watering is essential during the first few weeks, or all your efforts will be wasted. Table 7 outlines the general types of grass available. Select the seed mixture based on what function you want your lawn to perform, and buy good quality seed.

Whether composed of inert materials or plants, floors are vital to the landscape. The part they play in conserving moisture, suppressing weeds and erosion control means that their condition affects other elements in the garden. Not only do they require specific maintenance, their integrated role in the landscape means that they can also affect maintenance overall.

CHAPTER 5

Transitions

I n planning a garden, the first efforts are devoted to the basic structure—ceilings, walls, and floors—and these will create a garden that is almost complete. To take away the rough edges, blend the various parts and create a sense of unity, some thought must be given to transitions between rooms and elements.

When home owners turn to landscaping, one of the first projects they undertake, and sometimes the only one, is foundation planting. These are the plants positioned close to a house that help to soften its outline and tie it to the landscape, thereby creating a transition between house and yard. There are other transition areas in a landscape, however, that are often overlooked. These include transitions between house and deck, between deck and ground, between public and private areas of a yard and between different kinds of vegetation. The effect of a smooth change from one structure or area to another gives a landscape design a finished, unified look. A proper foundation planting can help reduce heating costs; plantings around a deck can bring fragrance and beauty to a summer's evening and hide unattractive support structures; and paths can lead one on a tour of mystery, surprise and discovery in a garden.

The effect of a smooth change from one structure or area to another gives a landscape design a finished, unified look.

❧ Between Structures and the Landscape

The most difficult transition is between man-made structures and the landscape. Plants alone might be used to provide a transition in such areas, such as a foundation planting. Structures themselves might serve as a transition, as in verandahs and arcades next to buildings. Plants and structures together can also help, as in a vine-covered walkway or a paved patio with plants between the cracks.

Plants

Plants alone are often used next to a free-standing wall or against the foundation of a house to ease the change between a flat stretch of lawn and an abrupt, vertical structure.

Depending on how much space is available, the plants can be one, two, or three layers deep. The important point to keep in mind is that the heights of the plants should vary.

It is also a help to have taller plants at the ends or corners, especially where houses are concerned, with lower plants towards the middle. Too often, tall plants are positioned on either side of a front door. In that situation the eye is drawn towards the tall plants, and then wanders away from the front door towards smaller plants and objects. Small specimen plants or intermediate-sized plants are best placed by a doorway; this helps to give a sense of welcome. Against a freestanding wall, the focus, instead of being a doorway, could be a prized plant, a water fountain or a statue.

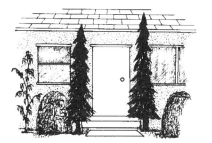 

Where there is a deck, the same principles apply. Too often the existing foundation planting is never extended around the deck. If the deck is very high and supported on tall pillars, vines can be used to tie it to the ground, or plant small trees and tall shrubs next to the deck.

If you have very limited space for a foundation planting, you might want to use vines or wall shrubs or the espalier technique discussed in Chapter 3. Even if you have a lot of space, the effects of filtered light created by leaves around the edge of a window can be very charming. Wall shrubs or vines planted next to a window help to bring the outdoors in and create beautiful effects of dappled light and arching branches. Keep in mind the heights of plants positioned there. Foundation plants have a way of growing up over windows and burying the house in a jungle of foliage.

One advantage of a good foundation planting is the potential for winter energy savings, particularly against north, east and west walls. Storms often roar in from the northwest, and sometimes from the south, but local conditions can alter this so check at your own location. Needled evergreens are very

1—When planning foundation plantings, avoid tall plants next to entries, where they may look forbidding and will become a nuisance.
2—Make entries highly visible by using low to medium sized plants, which help to give a welcoming look. Build up to taller plants at the corners of buildings.

effective, especially on the windward side, but deciduous shrubs can also create a dead air space. In restricted spaces, deciduous vines can be used. Evergreen vines are good on a northern exposure but would probably not be able to withstand harsh winters. The aim is to keep warm air in and cold air out, thereby reducing the internal/external differential. Wind is the greatest heat thief, and creating a dead air-space next to a house can reduce heating costs by as much as twenty-five percent in windy sites.

There are, however, certain difficulties in growing plants right next to a house. Conditions are almost certainly dry, and construction rubble is often buried next to the house. There are extremes of light, shade, coolness and heat, and the corners of buildings and freestanding walls can be extremely windy.

Foundation plantings can be used to balance the shape of a house. A low, narrow house, for example, can be lent height and width with small to medium sized trees planted at the sides. A tall, upright house can be tied to the surrounding landscape with a broad, rounded foundation planting.

To counteract these problems, plant shrubs and vines no closer than 50 cm from any wall, and direct the roots outwards away from the wall. Heat leaking from a house foundation can kill a plant because it isn't able to go into dormancy properly. For tender, broad-leaved evergreens the extra heat can be an advantage. Ideally, shrubs should be planted so that, after reaching their ultimate size, their branches are 50 cm away from the wall. For example, if a shrub has an ultimate spread of 2 m, it should be planted 1.5 m away from the house (half its ultimate spread, plus 0.5 m). That way the plants are not misshapen from growing cramped up against a wall, and house maintenance is easier because there is room to walk between the shrubs and the house. To give you some idea of the ultimate spread of a plant, compare its shape to its height. If a plant is rounded, its ultimate spread will be approximately equal to its height; if it is upright or vase

shaped, its ultimate spread will be somewhat less than its height; and a spreading plant will be broader than its height.

Working in lots of compost and well-rotted manure will also help to counteract dryness. False Cypress (*Chamaecyparis*), Cedar (*Thuja*), and the broad-leaved evergreens require moist soils. This can be difficult to maintain next to foundations, so work in plenty of organic matter, water regularly the first two or three years, and mulch with 8 cm to 10 cm of shredded bark. Fir and Spruce need moist soils to a lesser extent, and Pine, Yew and Juniper, once established, can tolerate drought. For all plants, water well for the first two or three years; water evergreens deeply and thoroughly and mulch before freeze-up each autumn.

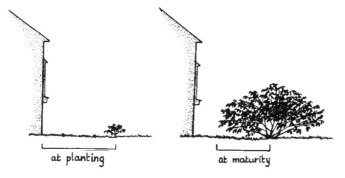

at planting at maturity

Foundation plants must be placed far enough from the house to provide room for uninhibited spread at maturity. This also puts the plant away from the zone of dry soil next to foundations, and allows room for easy maintenance of the house.

While you are digging good wide planting holes and working in all this wonderful organic matter, you will probably find buried building rubble. Remove as much of this as possible and be sure to check the soil pH and nutrient content. Soil next to buildings is often alkaline and high in calcium, so choose your plants accordingly, or else lower the pH with ground sulphur, iron sulphate or ammonium sulphate.

An advantage of this microclimate is in planting broad-leaved evergreens where they will get sun in summer and shade in winter. A good place is out some distance from north-facing walls; the high angle of summer sun will give them lots of light, and the low angle of winter sun will keep them in shade, reducing their need for moisture. This will help to reduce damage from winter drought. They would also do well against an east-facing wall. For problems associated with extremes of light, shade, coolness and heat, see Chapter 3.

Increased wind speeds next to buildings can completely ruin some plants. Of particular importance is the need to keep broad-leaved evergreens, such as Box, Hollies and Rhododendrons, away from the corners of buildings where wind speeds are greatest. This will also help to reduce damage from winter drought.

You might find that there are some very sheltered areas next to walls that are ideal for tender plants. You can find the right places by tying strips of cloth or plastic to sticks and placing them at intervals around the foundation or against a garden wall. Areas of snow buildup will also indicate sheltered spots. Have you ever noticed how the ground is often swept bare of snow at the corners of buildings and piled up next to steps? Table 8 lists wind-sensitive and wind-tolerant plants.

Transition Structures and Plants

Structures as well as plants can act as transition elements in the landscape. Along the edge of a building seems an ideal place to sit, lean or walk, and the structures we often find there help to soften and blur the distinction between indoors and outdoors. Steps, verandahs, decks, patios and covered

This deck, as well as the steps and flagstone path, provide a transition zone between the house and garden. The plants enhance the move from indoors to out and make the deck into a delightful room with living walls. It is important to carry the foundation planting around the base of the deck, as has been begun here with a young planting by the steps.

walkways stretch the indoors to the outdoors; plants used in conjunction with these structures help to bring the outdoors in.

Consider a deck, for example. If you relate the house to the deck, and relate the deck to the landscape, moving between the house and the landscape is smoother and gives the house and garden a wholeness and unity.

There are little tricks to tie a house to the deck (or steps, verandah, patio or walkway). The most obvious one is to use the same materials in construction. If your deck is already built and doesn't match the house, you might be able to use some of the house materials for trimming the deck. An example would be brick edgings for a stone patio built next to a brick house, or wooden edgings if next to a wooden house. Using similar flooring materials for the outdoor area and the adjoining room can also be effective, such as hardwood floors next to a wooden deck, or paving tiles for indoors and out. Putting the deck on the same level as the floor in the house is another way of easing the transition. Colour, too, can do a lot to relate outside structures to a building. Red trim on a house, for example, can be matched with red furniture or red planters on the deck or patio. Similar furniture for indoors and out, such as wicker or wooden furniture, is another way to ensure a smooth transition.

You don't necessarily have to have a deck or patio to make a smooth transition from indoors to out. Some of these suggestions could also be applied to other outdoor structures. A walkway next to the house could be covered with a trellis to form an open, airy arcade, giving a feeling of special protection and intimacy, half indoors and half out. Wide, generous steps can lead directly from the house to the garden, creating a warm invitation to sit a while. A sturdy tree can have seating arranged at the base, and a grassy area can have furniture that matches indoor or deck furniture in style or colour.

Plants are perhaps the most effective way of blurring the edges especially as some of the methods mentioned above may not be suitable to your situation. If you have a patio door, or a window overlooking the garden, you could arrange houseplants around it indoors so that you look out through a frame of foliage. You might even have some potted plants just outside the doors on the deck or landing or stairs. Incorporating planters in your deck design for growing herbs can bring the garden a little closer. You could have pots of flowers or foliage wandering down the steps and out onto the grass. Draping and trailing plants help to blur and soften the edges of planters.

If you have stepping stones, brick paths or a paved patio leading to your garden, you can make the boundary between constructed and natural elements more ambiguous by leaving cracks for small plants. Spaces between the bricks or stones can get larger, and the paving elements more scattered as the distance from the house increases. You could even leave proper planting holes in a patio by leaving out paving stones or blocks of bricks, with a few small holes close to the house and larger and more frequent ones near the garden. Sun lovers for this purpose include the following:

Arabis	*Draba*	*Sempervivum*
Arenaria	*Iberis*	*(Hen-and-Chickens)*
Artemisia	*Phlox (Moss Pink)*	*Thrift (Armeria)*
Basket-of-Gold	*Potentilla*	*Thyme, creeping*
Dianthus (Pinks)	*Sedum*	

Beauties for shady spots include:

Arenaria	*Chamomile*	*Saxifrage*
Bluets	*Coralbells*	*Sweet Woodruff*
Bugleweed	*Ferns*	*Violets*
Campanula	*Fringed Bleeding Heart*	

The only caution in using this approach is to make sure the planting area is completely free of weeds before setting in your plants. It is next to impossible to weed effectively once the plants are in.

✑ Paths for Transition

Often there needs to be a transition between different areas of a garden, and paths most often serve this function. There is an appeal to thoughtfully considered and carefully laid out garden paths. They lead one on to discover the secrets and delights that are hidden and tucked away, just around the next corner.

The logical way to plan a path is to look at the natural points of interest, and then connect them following natural ground contours. A goal, or point of interest, could be a tree, fountain, seat, swing, statue, entrance, patio and so on. These are the interesting goals. There are also the mundane service areas, such as compost heap and garden shed which must be reached. It is possible to arrange the service path off to one side of the yard, or else have the service area off to one side of a path but not at the end of it.

One thing to not do is to run a path through the middle of a yard, unless you do it carefully. A path running lengthwise through the middle of a long, narrow city lot will only accentuate its shape. Off to one side is a slightly better proposition. The best solution, however, is to have the path start off on one side, cross over to the other side, and carry on down. Breaking up the length of the lot by crossing over shortens that dimension.

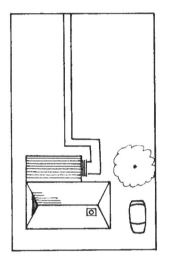 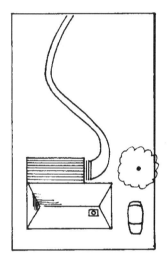

Avoid tight, angular turns in paths (left), which encourage people to take shortcuts. Paths should curve gently and follow natural contours (right).

You might choose to have a path terminate at the point of interest, such as a path going to a secluded patio or a view of the ocean, or you might want your paths to form one circuit. It is a good idea to put a wider area in the middle of a path where you have your deck or children's play area or back step seat. This is an invitation to stop awhile to sit or do or be.

Where two paths cross, you could place a special feature, such as a bird bath or garden seat or statue. Put it between the two paths close to the intersection, so that pedestrians can walk unimpeded, with an easy view from either path.

Paths can be straight or curved. Businesslike ones, such as those that reach service areas, are usually straight. One doesn't usually wander through the garden to put out the garbage, unless the path also serves to divide the garden or is a means to navigate the garden. Gently curving paths that wind around flower beds, ponds and shrub borders seem more suited to the leisurely pace and environment of the backyard. To further encourage a leisurely pace, use short plants set back from the path. Tall plants set close to the path urge a faster pace. If you decide to put in curves, make them gradual, and try to follow natural contours. Too sharp a curve will simply encourage users to take shortcuts, especially where pedestrian traffic comes off the street.

If you are having trouble deciding where to put a path, watch a while to see where people normally walk. Sometimes a path is so well used and so well placed that a building project is designed to take it into consideration, such as a deck with a corner left off to keep the path on its course. This also helps the new structure become part of the landscape.

Once you have settled on the course the path will take, you might be interested in subtle variations that can be incorporated in the design. These methods of transition will give gentle, unobtrusive hints that a user is moving into other areas of the garden. Consider a path that moves from street to front door. Something about the path, or the area immediately adjacent to the path, must change: light, sound, direction, surface, level, width, or enclosure.

Light and sound levels can be altered by leading the path through a group of shrubs, perhaps part of the foundation planting as one approaches the front door. The path might

Widen paths at points of interest to encourage people to slow down and pause a while.

simply turn direction; instead of travelling in one straight line from street to door, the path can take a gentle turn as it nears the door. The surface of the path itself might change, from plain concrete to stones set in concrete, for example. The level of the path can be changed, going up two or more steps at the point where you wish to create a sense of privacy. The path can also be made narrower where the semi-private or private area begins, narrowing from 1.5 m to 1 m. Paths as narrow as 0.5 m should be used in only the most secluded areas. Some form of enclosure, such as a gate or archway or trellised walk, can also create a sense that one is moving into a private area. A gate, in fact, need not be part of a fence; it can be supported by posts set into a bed of shrubs and seem a natural and normal element.

Changes in a path give gentle hints that one is approaching a private part of the garden.

These same principles can be applied to paths anywhere in the garden, and we often use them without even realizing it. We take a couple of steps up or down when moving off the patio, or create a sense of privacy by turning a path around a shrub border, or change the path surface from concrete to logs to bark as a path travels from house to woods. Designing path layouts and playing with transition techniques is not only fun, it makes your yard a garden of subtlety and delight.

In order that the path brings pleasure and not more work once it is completed, a little consideration should be given to maintenance. Concrete paths must be properly installed; brick or stone paths must be carefully laid in a weed-free, well-drained bed; wooden boardwalks must have dry, well-drained beds; and surfaces must be shaped so that water doesn't collect after rain. If heavy plastic or tar paper is used underneath to keep down weeds, it should be punched at 30 cm intervals to allow drainage. It helps to have the surface at the right height for lawn mowing so that the wheels of the mower can ride on the path, giving a relatively neat, care-free edge.

Driveway Transitions

Driveways are also paths, and the principles for placing them on a large property follow the same as for paths. The trees and shrubs planted along lengthy driveways can give subtle clues about approaching changes in the road. Plantings on the outside of curves tell of an approaching change in direction. If trees are regularly spaced for most of the distance, but planted closer together as an intersection is approached, drivers will tend to slow down. Another hint that an intersection is near is broader plantings of trees and shrubs, with more rows of plants. Right at the intersection, the plantings should open up completely to give a clear line of vision in every direction.

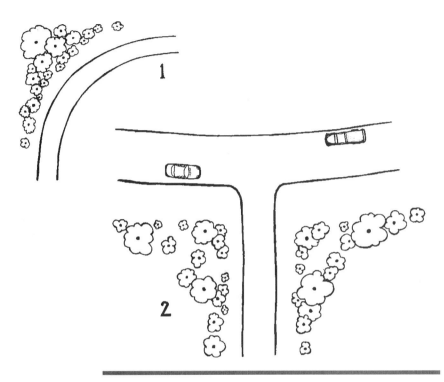

1—Plants on the outside of a curve indicate a change of direction. 2—Trees planted in wider arrangements indicate that an intersection is near; keep visibility clear at the intersection. 3—Alternatively, on long driveways, space trees or shrubs progressively closer to slow traffic as busy roads are approached. (On winding roads, or where a driveway is broadside to the wind, trees should be set back 20 m to 25 m from the road.)

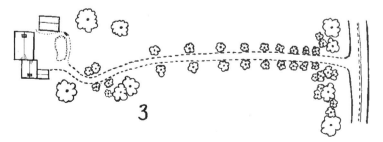

✒ Transitions in Vegetation

Transitions in vegetation can take several forms, including formal to informal, short to tall, cultivated to wild or natural, open to woodland, adult to child-oriented and sunny to shady. It is impossible to discuss every case, but some examples might indicate the sorts of things to consider.

The underlying principle is to use vegetation that is intermediate between the two extremes. If you have a shrub border, for example, that is in full sun at one end and in considerable shade at the other, you would plant sun-loving shrubs at one end, shade-tolerant shrubs at the other, and shrubs that tolerate both sun and shade, throughout the border. That way, there is no abrupt change between one type of vegetation and the other.

Suppose you like the trim neatness of a formal garden, but realize that you haven't the time to keep the entire garden to that level of care; you could choose to have a quite formal arrangement next to the house, with neatly clipped hedges, symmetrical beds, and a carefully manicured lawn. This would gradually give way to a shrub border or unclipped hedge, using in part the same plant that forms the formal hedge. Boxwood, for example, is usually seen in a formal setting, but if left unclipped it forms interesting mounds. The lawn could change to a rough lawn and then perhaps to a meadow if there is enough space. Even flower shape could change, as in roses that progress from hybrid teas in the formal setting, to multi-petalled shrub roses, to singles at the informal end of the garden. Hybrid teas would look out of place at the edge of a meadow and single roses seem a poor cousin in a formal setting, but by using roses this way, a rose theme is carried throughout the garden and the transition from formal to informal is gradual.

Let us imagine now that you have a landscaped garden backing onto a woodland. The garden would probably be

Flower form can be used as a transition element between informal and formal areas of the garden: roses, left to right, are single, semi-double, and double.

planted with cultivated trees and shrubs, and you wish to make a smooth transition to the wild, native, uncultivated plants. In this situation you would use trees and shrubs that seem at home in either setting, mixing them with plants in the wild and cultivated areas, and using them alone in the zone between the two areas.

Such trees would include:

Alternate-Leaf Dogwood	*Eastern Redbud*
Amelanchier	*European Mtn. Ash*
Amur Maple	*Gray (River) Birch*
Bird (Pin) Cherry	*Hawthorns*
Chinese Flowering Dogwood	*Mountain Maple*
Choke Cherry	*Striped Maple*
Cornelian Cherry	*White Cedar (Thuja)*
Crabapples	

Large shrubs of suitable transition material include:

Azalea	*Nannyberry*
Canada Holly	*Ninebark*
Elderberry	*Pieris*
Hazelnut	*Red Chokeberry*
Highbush Blueberry	*Rhododendrons*
Highbush Cranberry	*Sorbaria*
Hydrangea arborescens	*Snowball Viburnum*
Leucothoe	*Wayfaring Tree*
Mountain Holly	*Witch Hazel*
Mountain Laurel	*Witherod*

Some suitable smaller plants are:

Bearberry	*Lambkill*
Bog Rosemary	*Mayflower*
Canada Yew	*Meadowsweet*
Cinquefoil	*Rhodora canadense*
Ferns	*Sweetfern*

Huckleberry   *Wintergreen*
Juniper (low forms)

Many of these trees and shrubs are native in eastern Canada or are plants that are native to the eastern United States. Some Rhododendrons, for example, are found in open woodlands in their natural settings and are very effective as transition plants.

As to growing conditions, most of these plants are quite happy in partial shade, although several will tolerate or are happier in full sun, such as:

Birch   *Juniper*
Chokeberry   *Meadowsweet*
Cinquefoil   *Nannyberry*
Elderberry   *Ninebark*
Hawthorn   *Snowball Viburnum*
Highbush Cranberry   *Sweetfern*
Hydrangea   *Wayfaring Tree*

Some of these can tolerate quite wet conditions, although none like standing water, and these include:

Canada Holly   *Mountain Maple*
Elderberry   *Nannyberry*
Highbush Cranberry   *Snowball Viburnum*
Meadowsweet   *Witherod*
Mountain Ash

Another transition that sometimes occurs is from very open areas to woodlands. The plants mentioned above would be quite effective as transition material, but it would be good to consider their position as well. They should be planted so that the size of the plants gradually decreases, from woodland to open area. A few isolated trees or individual shrubs could also be planted in the lawn, blurring the distinction between open and wooded areas, although this would make mowing more difficult.

Transitions in a garden can be of many forms. In order to determine what kinds you need, consider the various parts and pieces of your garden, and then work out suitable transitions between them.

CHAPTER 6

Growing Conditions

Providing the right growing conditions for your garden treasures is such an obvious investment to make, but it often receives only cursory consideration. We know that plants need air, light, nutrients and moisture to grow properly, but we sometimes forget that providing the right conditions also enables plants to resist pests and disease and to produce more and bigger flowers and fruits. Your visitors may not notice such subtleties as plant shape and foliage colour, or a cleverly designed walkway, but they will most certainly notice plants that are badly damaged by pest insects, disease or environmental stresses. It is also costly in time, energy and money to fuss over diseased plants or to move or replace inappropriate plants. It is so much easier to consider growing conditions before the first plant is ever put in the ground.

> We sometimes forget that providing the right conditions enables plants to resist pests and disease and to produce more and bigger flowers and fruits.

Considering the air, light, nutrient and moisture needs of plants, gardeners can exert direct control over some aspects of the growing conditions, and only indirect or incomplete control over other aspects.

✍§ Air, Temperature and Wind

The annual temperature range, windiness, local air circulation, air in the soil, air pollution and salt spray all affect plant growth. Not much can be done about the hardiness zone with which you are blessed or cursed, but you can use your ingenuity to work around the situation. If you live in zone 5, for example, you may have sheltered areas that are effectively a zone 6, or frost pockets and windy areas that are effectively a zone 4.

Some shrubs for which a certain hardiness rating has been given will tolerate colder conditions but will usually have some dieback. Shrub roses, for example, will sometimes be killed back to the ground, but they grow well and recuperate readily each spring. Leucothoe, normally considered a tender, medium-sized shrub in zone 6, will die back but survive in zone 4 and can function effectively as a low-growing groundcover. The dieback that these and other shrubs experience can be viewed as self-pruning that encourages young, vigorous growth. Other shrubs, such as Azaleas, will survive colder zones than recommended, but it is their flower buds which are not as hardy and need a warmer zone. To help plants harden off for the winter, keep deciduous shrubs on the dry side in autumn, and withhold fertilizer after mid-July. Plants that bloom in very early spring need extra shelter so that their buds are not nipped by frost. It helps as well to plant them where they do not receive early morning sun, so that their flower buds thaw slowly.

Trees are such a big investment that you will want to be very careful to choose ones that are well-suited to your zone, but you might be more inclined to take a gamble with less costly shrubs or perennials that are of borderline hardiness. This is especially true if you know you have sheltered places for those or are keen to try unusual plants. You can even go to the extreme of using winter mulches of oak leaves or evergreen boughs, and burlap barriers for your tender specimens.

Wind affects plant hardiness, but nevertheless air circulation is important in disease control. Moulds, mildews and other fungal diseases thrive in cramped city gardens and areas where air circulation is poor. To reduce disease problems and the time spent treating them, space your plants farther apart, thin and prune branches, plant resistant varieties, use raised beds, destroy affected fruit and leaves, remove old mulch and rake the ground around your plants, applying new mulch after shoots appear in spring, and always water from underneath so that water doesn't stay on the leaves unnecessarily.

Plants also need air in the soil in order to grow properly. If soil is waterlogged or compacted, or if it has been subjected to the use of plastic mulches, the cause of death or poor growth in plants is usually lack of air for the roots. Organic matter keeps the soil light enough to retain air.

Air pollution is a problem in some areas. Using plants with smooth leaves, rather than hairy or crinkly, and ensuring that all the needs of plants are well met will help plants resist pollution. For severe problems, pollution resistant plants would be in order, and these are listed here in increasing order of height:

English Ivy	*Honey-Locust*
Climbing Hydrangea	*Green Ash*
Goldenrain Tree	*Ginkgo*

Ruby Horse Chestnut	*Colorado Spruce*
Hackberry	*Five-Leaved Aralia*
Common Horse Chestnut	*Bradford Callery Pear*
Pin Oak	*Amur Cork Tree*
Garland Spirea	*Austrian Pine*
Russian Olive	*Sycamore Maple*
Little Leaf Linden	*Norway Maple*

Trees that are particularly sensitive to pollution include:

American Linden	*Hemlock*
American Beech	*Red Maple*
Birch	*Sugar Maple*
European Larch	

Salt spray is an airborne problem affecting plants growing by the coast or next to city streets where salt is used on ice and snow in winter. Salt can also get into the soil and disturb plant root systems, and plants have different tolerances. Thuja, for example, can tolerate salt in the root zone but not on its foliage, and Spruce can tolerate salt spray on its foliage but not salt in the soil. Yew can tolerate ocean spray but not salty street slush. If plants do suffer salt damage, the affected foliage can sometimes be trimmed off in spring. If salt in the soil is a problem, especially along city streets, flush the soil thoroughly in spring with plenty of water.

Some annual and perennial flowers that tolerate coastal conditions include:

Armeria	*Dianthus*	*Rudbeckia*
Artemisia	*Dusty Miller*	*Salvia*
Begonia	*Gaillardia*	*Shasta Daisy*
Calendula	*Hollyhock*	*Statice*
Carnation	*Iberis*	*Stock*
Centaurea	*Lamb's Ear*	*Sunflower*
Chrysanthemum	*Marigold*	*Sweet Alyssum*
Cranesbill	*Petunia*	*Verbena*
Daylily	*Portulaca*	*Veronica*
Delphinium	*Primula*	*Zinnia*

A crude guideline is that drought-tolerant plants seem to be also salt-tolerant.

✑ Light

Once the air needs of plants have been taken care of, the light requirements can be considered. Again, you probably have very little control over how much sun your garden receives, but there are lots of things you can do to work around the situation.

The first is to realize with what kind of shade you are dealing. If you have an area that receives a minimum of 8 hours sun each day, you can consider it full sun, even though it receives full or partial shade for part of each day. If you have an area that receives at least 4 hours of direct sunlight each day, or is in light, dappled shade most of the time, then you have partial shade. New gardeners sometimes feel that only shade-loving plants can grow in partial shade, but that is in fact not the case, especially if other plant needs are considered. What makes partial shade particularly difficult is if plants are shaded in the morning and then suddenly exposed to scorching noonday sun. Shade on the north side of a building or shadows cast by tall buildings or large dense trees is full shade, restricting the choice of plants. In this situation, there might still be enough indirect sunlight, or sky shine, for some species. The shade found under coniferous trees is often too dense for all but a few native plants, and is best avoided by gardeners.

Once you have realized the kind of shade you have, the second point to understand in shade gardening is that plant failures are due more to lack of moisture, fertility and air movement than lack of light. There are four basic practices to help ensure successful shade gardening. Mostly they refer to the situation under trees, but the principles apply as well to shade cast by buildings. First, space your plants further apart than usual. This will compensate for drier conditions, poor air circulation and reduced light. Second, improve the soil fertility by working in plenty of organic matter. Work in pockets of rich soil between roots, and fertilize regularly. Third, water deeply and regularly, especially in the first two or three years of a planting, and mulch to conserve moisture. The soil under trees and next to buildings is often very dry because rain cannot reach it. Fourth, increase the light if possible. Trunks of deciduous trees can be cleared of branches up to a height of 10 m on a large tree, and tree canopies can be thinned. This alone might take you from a full to a partial shade situation, and will certainly increase the amount of light in a partial shade setting. You might be able to paint an offending building or wall in a light colour, thereby brightening a shady area quickly and easily.

If you make an accurate assessment of the kind of shade you have, and if you can improve the availability of air, nutrients and moisture to plants to compensate for reduced light, then you will certainly be on the road to successful gardening in the shade. To illustrate these points, it might help to consider some of the planting situations you may face, and to give you some ideas of what to try in your garden.

Growing lawns in shade is difficult, but the following tips help: plant shade-tolerant grasses such as tall fescues, or plant a mixture and let the grasses fight it out; fertilize with utmost regularity, spring and fall; fertilize lawn trees deeply; maintain soil pH of 6.3 to 6.7; raise cutting height 25% to 50% because it makes sparse grass look thicker; and mow less frequently to compensate for the slower growth rate. If these measures fail, consider a mulch of pebbles or shredded bark, or use shade-tolerant groundcover plants.

There are many perennial flowers that will tolerate moderately shady settings, including beebalm (below). Plants grown in shade suffer more from lack of moisture, fertility and air movement than lack of light. After growing conditions are considered, choose plants on the basis of other desirable characteristics. Beebalm, for example, creates interest in several seasons for its leaves, flowers and seed heads as well as being attractive to desirable visitors, such as hummingbirds.

If you want to grow flowers in a woodland setting, there are many choices for shade. The first step is to clear the underbrush, thin out crowded saplings, and then prune and trim trees as described above. Spring flowering bulbs often do well under trees because they do most of their growing before the trees leaf out. Particularly shade tolerant bulbs and tuberous roots include Anemone, Hardy Cyclamen, Trout Lily, Fritillaria, Snowdrops, Grape Hyacinth, Scilla and Virginia

Bluebells. It also helps to work in extra compost after they flower. Summer tubers, such as Caladium, Calla Lily, and Tuberous Begonia, can be planted directly in the soil in full or partial shade, or set out in pots among groundcover plants. Wildflowers can be used, as long as growing conditions identical to their natural setting can be provided. If rescuing wildflowers from construction sites, dig up as large a volume of soil as possible around each plant.

Many perennial flowers are suitable as well (those marked with * are worth trying in nearly sunless positions):

*Ajuga	*Foamflower	*Meadow rue
Arabis	Foxglove	Meadowsweet
*Aruncus	Gasplant	Oenothera
Aster	Globeflower	Pansy
Astilbe	Helleborus	Phlox
*Beebalm	Hepatica	Primula
*Bleeding Hearts	*Hosta	*Pulmonaria
Campanula	Iberis	Saxifrage
*Columbine	Impatiens	*Solomon's Seal
Coralbells	Jacob's Ladder	Sweet Woodruff
Daylily	*Lamium	*Trillium
Delphinium	*Lily-of-the Valley	Violet
Fibrous Begonia	*Lobelia	Wild Ginger

There are even roses that can be grown in some shade. The Rugosa roses and their hybrids tolerate moderate shade, and many roses will do well if they get early morning sun and good air circulation. The sunshine and air are important for drying off foliage quickly so that diseases do not develop.

Ferns seem a natural for shady conditions, although they must have some sunlight to do well, especially when they are young and getting established. What they do not like is scorching noonday sun and drying winds. They must never dry out, but that is not a problem if mulch and compost are used. Do your weeding and spring clean up by hand so that the shallow root systems and tender fiddleheads are not harmed.

You can use ferns in more than just woodland settings. They can be used in large groupings along the house foundation as long as they are kept moist, as groundcovers, as individual accents with shrubs or cultivated flowers and as a background for flower borders. Fiddleheads look perfect with spring flowering bulbs, and fern fronds later hide maturing bulb leaves, or imagine ferns with a background of Azaleas. Try mixing them with Astilbe, or contrast them with the smooth, broad leaves of Hosta. Ferns help to lighten heavy masses, such as boulders, Rhododendrons, and walls, they are charming along walks, and they work well to define paths and portions of a yard.

Evergreen ferns, such as Rock Polypody, Crested Shield, Marginal, and Christmas Fern, are ideally placed where they can be seen in winter, and they can be brightened up by trimming back the older foliage after their spring flush. Rampant, invasive ferns should only be used as groundcovers in large areas or under trees or where they can be carefully restricted, perhaps with metal or plastic edging. These include Hay-Scented, Lady, Bracken and Sensitive Fern. Ferns are wonderfully versatile and can be used in so many ways throughout a garden that their use ought to be encouraged.

It is even possible to grow vegetables in a shady yard. Root and leaf crops, such as carrots, turnips, lettuce and cabbage, require less light than fruit and flower crops, such as tomatoes, squashes, strawberries and broccoli. If you want to go to the trouble, sun-loving plants can be grown in containers and moved throughout the day to follow the path of the sun. Currants, gooseberries and blueberries can all tolerate partial shade, although fruit production might be lower. Remember, though, to be generous with the moisture and provide adequate nutrients.

Pay attention to local environmental conditions when planning the vegetable garden. For example, root crops and leafy green vegetables tolerate some shade, but fruit producing crops, such as tomatoes, require at least 8 hours of sunshine each day.

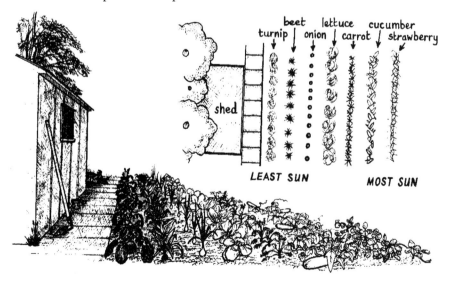

beet lettuce cucumber
turnip | onion | carrot | strawberry

shed

LEAST SUN   MOST SUN

Most herbs like full sun, but several will tolerate some degree of shade. They include:

Angelica	*Lemon Balm*	*Sweet Cicely*
Catnip	*Lemon Verbena*	*Sweet Woodruff*
Chamomile	*Lovage*	*Tarragon*
Chervil	*Marjoram*	*Wild Ginger*
Costmary	*Mint*	*Winter Savory*
Curly Parsley	*Oregano*	

So much can be accomplished in shady gardens that they ought to be considered treasures instead of burdens. Simply remembering the basic needs of plants is the secret of success.

Sometimes the light requirements of plants vary from summer to winter. This is particularly so with broad-leaved evergreens. In summer, Rhododendrons, Mountain Laurel, Holly and Boxwood do well in partial sun, or in full sun if they are kept moist. An eastern exposure is good, but in a south or western exposure they should be shaded by a tree, particularly at noon. Where summers are particularly warm, the high overhead shade provided by large trees is ideal. In winter, plants will suffer from not being able to obtain moisture from the frozen ground. This shows up in spring as browning of foliage and possibly dieback. A burlap barrier is effective at protecting against drying winter winds.

One solution is to position plants so that they receive sun in summer and shade in winter. This can be on the north, northwest or northeast side of a house or wall or row of conifers. The overhead sun of summer will reach them, but not the low-angled sun of winter.

If evergreens do brown in spite of your care, wait until new growth starts before pruning out what seem to be dead branches. New growth will sometimes start from the branch tips, and two-year-old needles and leaves fall off naturally anyway.

✍ Nutrients

Having considered the air and light requirements of plants, consider next their nutrient needs. Soil is an important investment when you think that fully half of every shrub and blade of grass is hidden from view, bound to the earth with an extensive root system.

It is organic particles in the soil that bind and retain the necessary nutrients. If synthetic fertilizers are relied on, then more and more fertilizer must be used as the nutrients leach away faster and faster because of dwindling supplies of organic matter. Synthetic fertilizers also make the environment unsuitable for soil micro-organisms. It is these micro-organisms that break down the organic matter, releasing nutrients. They also facilitate uptake of nutrients by plant roots, and some of them, found throughout the soil, fix nitrogen. In addition, some micro-organisms bind soil particles together, thereby reducing erosion.

Organic matter has to be added continually to the soil to keep up the supply. It comes in many forms; rotted leaves, well-rotted manure, compost, and nearly any other aged organic material can be worked into the soil. Avoid using peat moss, as it is a natural resource that cannot be replaced readily in any given location. The annual cycle of root regeneration adds organic matter naturally. Mulches, such as pine needles, shredded bark and sawdust, also add organic matter to the soil. They use up nitrogen in the breakdown process, however, so it is a good idea to sprinkle in some 10-10-10 fertilizer or lots of fresh grass clippings with the mulch. Organic fertilizers, such as bone meal, are slower to release their nutrients than synthetic fertilizers, so they should be added to soil several months before plants need them. Some faster acting organic fertilizers include green plant material, seaweed, dried blood, fish emulsion and wood ashes. They should all be worked into the soil before planting, especially wood ashes which can harm plants if in direct contact with them. Organic fertilizers are preferable to synthetic fertilizers, even though they are sometimes more expensive. Compost is organic matter and fertilizer rolled into one and costs nothing.

In spite of your care in supplying nutrients to plants, there might be situations where you need plants that can tolerate poor soils. Some perennial flowers for poor conditions include:

Achillea(Yarrow)	*Coreopsis*	*Oenothera*
Aubrieta	*Cranesbill*	*Rudbeckia*
Baby's Breath	*Daylily*	*Salvia*
Campanula	*Dianthus*	*Sedum*
Catnip	*Forget-me-not*	*Sempervivum*
Cerastium	*Foxglove*	*Thyme, creeping*
Chinese Lantern	*Gaillardia*	*Wallflower*
Columbine	*Phlox (Moss Pink)*	

Gardeners hear a lot about soil pH, but there isn't much said about why it is important. The main difficulty is with nutrient availability. If soil is too alkaline (pH above 7.0), trace elements are locked up and salt concentration increases. If soil is too acidic, phosphorous is in an unusable form, and calcium, potassium, and magnesium all leach out faster. Earthworms leave and soil bacteria slow down, so less humus is produced, and clubroot disease is more likely.

Most plants grow quite well in the 6.0 to 7.0 range but some grow better, or at least will tolerate, very acidic or alkaline conditions. Table 11 lists common plants and their preferred pH range. Note that many plants which prefer or tolerate lime will also grow in somewhat acidic conditions. As well, moisture loving plants generally prefer acidic conditions. It cuts down on maintenance time if plants with similar pH requirements can be grouped together.

Soil pH can be determined by using readily available pH test kits. Old timers tasted the soil to test acidity, and weeds are also an indicator. Acidic soils support Red (Sheep) Sorrel, Stinking Mayweed and Plantain.

If soil is alkaline, pH can be lowered by using sawdust, pine needles and shredded bark as mulches or soil amendments (remember to add a little nitrogen). Iron sulphate, ammonium sulphate (not aluminum sulphate) and ground sulphur worked into the soil will also increase acidity. Apply at a rate of 1 kg per 10 sq m. If your water is hard, using rain water on your plants will help to keep alkalinity from rising.

If soil is acidic, raise the pH by using bone meal, wood ashes, crushed eggshells and dolomitic limestone as soil amendments. Wood ashes can be applied at a rate of 1 kg per 10 square metres per year, or in one dose of 4 kg per l0 square metres. When you use limestone, apply it at a rate of 3.5 kg per 10 square metres, just before it rains, or wait two weeks before applying fertilizers, otherwise, the lime binds with the fertilizer, making it unavailable to plants. Lime has the side benefit of lightening heavy clay soils by binding the clay particles into larger particles. Wood ash neutralizes in a few weeks, whereas limestone takes 6 months to a year, and 1 part lime is equal to approximately 4 parts wood ash. To raise the pH and reduce the frequency of liming you might also want to stop using synthetic fertilizers, because they increase soil acidity. The use of synthetic fertilizers has been mentioned several times. Provided that the organic content of soil is maintained, synthetic fertilizers could be used with a light hand although their use should not be required with a good organic content in the soil. As well, they rely on fossil fuel for their production which might be offensive to some gardeners.

✌⅗ Water

The fourth basic requirement of plants is water. Water shortage is sometimes immediately obvious, as in wilting leaves. Sometimes the results show up several weeks after the fact, as in poor fruit production. On occasion, the effects of water shortage may not show up for several months when, for example, evergreens die in the spring after a dry winter, or spring flowering trees and shrubs fail to flower because of water shortage during bud production the previous year.

Organic matter in the soil is excellent at maintaining an even supply of moisture to plants. Water passes too quickly through sandy soils and too slowly through clay soils, but adding organic matter to either type improves the situation considerably. Use compost for small areas or rotted leaves for large areas. It is sometimes recommended to use sand to lighten clay soils, but huge amounts are required and the effect does not seem to be long lasting. Mulching is another effective means of maintaining an even moisture supply to plants and is discussed in the next section.

With consideration given to moist soils, rich in organic matter, there might still be situations that occur where poor conditions are not easily corrected, or where it makes more sense to use plants adapted to the existing growing conditions. Table 10 lists shrubs and trees suitable for sandy, clay, poor or dry soils.

Some flowers suited to sandy conditions include:

Achillea (Yarrow)	*Dianthus*	*Mesembryanthemum*
Baby's Breath	*Gladiolus*	*Tulip*
Carnation	*Hyacinth*	*Wallflower*
Crocus	*Iberis*	

Rudbeckia (also known as Brown-Eyed Susan, above) is a fairly drought tolerant plant. All such plants require regular watering while they are young and getting established. Extra organic matter in the soil aids moisture retention.

For flowers suited to, or tolerant of, clay conditions, try those in Chapter 8 recommended for wet conditions.

Note that many pines tolerate dry, sandy conditions, except Korean Pine. Broad-leaved evergreens are notoriously poor at tolerating drought, and it is difficult to find plants that tolerate both drought and shade. Many drought-tolerant plants are somewhat gray leaved, such as Butterfly Bush, Beauty Bush (*Kolkwitzia*), St. John's Wort, Lavender, and Rosemary. Even drought-tolerant plants need to be carefully watered the first two or three years, until they are well established. Drought-tolerant plants will eventually reduce maintenance, however, by demanding little or no watering time.

Some perennial flowers suited to dry conditions are:

Achillea (Yarrow)	*Chamomile*	*Phlox (Moss Pink)*
Arabis	*Coreopsis*	*Oriental Poppy*
Artemisia	*Cynoglossum*	*Pearly Everlasting*
Baby's Breath	*Dianthus*	*Purple Coneflower*
Bearded Iris	*Gaillardia*	*Rudbeckia*
Catnip	*Lamb's Ear*	*Sedum*
Centaurea	*Liatris*	*Thyme, creeping*

Plants grown in poor or dry soils will not reach the height and stature that they would on moist, fertile soils, but they often live longer.

If you do have wet, clay soils, stay off them in the spring until they are drier, and avoid working in the garden after summer rains. Rototillers are especially hard on clay soils and clay soils are hard on tillers, so be certain the soil has dried out sufficiently before tilling. Improving wet soils to help them drain more readily will help reduce the incidence of fungal diseases, such as leaf spot. Raised beds and planting trees and shrubs on a slight mound prevent roots from becoming waterlogged and suffocated. Table 12 lists shrubs and trees that will tolerate wet conditions.

For a full discussion of turning a difficult wet patch into an asset, and for further suggestions of suitable plants, see Water in Chapter 8.

✌§ Mulches

Mulches might be considered the fifth requirement for good plant growth. They regulate moisture, suppress weeds, add organic matter to the soil and control ground freezing in winter.

Mulches added to the soil surface help to regulate moisture. They do this by slowing down the rate of evaporation from the soil, and by suppressing the growth of weeds that compete for water and nutrients. Lip service is often given to mulching, but weeds are genuine threats to plants, not merely unsightly nuisances. Mulches also make weeds easier to pull out if they do grow, and help to maintain even soil temperatures. Dig out perennial weeds and hoe out the annual ones before applying mulches. It is also wise to wait until the soil has warmed up in spring; applying mulches too early prevents the soil from warming up and results in slower plant growth. Depending on the size of the plants, mulches from 5 cm to 10 cm deep can be applied, larger amounts for trees and shrubs and smaller amounts for small shrubs and herbaceous plants. Keep a cleared space around soft perennials because some soft-stemmed plants will rot if mulch is touching them.

There are many suitable mulches available. Aim for weed free, completely decomposed materials, although almost any mulch is better than no mulch. Some examples of mulches are:

- rotted manure (might contain weed seeds)
- shredded bark (excellent material, add nitrogen)
- sawdust or wood shavings (decompose slowly, add nitrogen)
- pine needles
- oak leaves (ideal as winter mulch because they don't pack down)
- shredded or rotted leaves (any sort, excellent)
- grass clippings (but best left on the lawn)
- straw (not hay as it is often full of weed seeds)
- compost

Gravel can also be used, as well as the new and expensive man-made sheet mulches. Peat moss is not very good as a mulch; once it dries out, water will not penetrate and it is very difficult to re-wet. It is also expensive if used over large areas. As to cost of other mulches, most are obtainable for free or a minimal fee. Try to buy in bulk, such as a truckload of shredded bark instead of several bags.

Living mulches can also be used. They are best planted two to three years after a new shrub or tree is planted and well established, but inert mulches can and should be used in the interim. Any of the perennial groundcover plants in Table 6 can be used.

Groundcover plants are not a good idea with perennial flowers, unless annuals are used as mulches. They are very effective, however, with spring flowering bulbs, as discussed in Chapter 4. A complete cover of shrubs is also very effective at maintaining soil moisture (and reducing weeds).

Winter mulches are essential for new plantings, some tender perennials and shrubs and both narrow and broad-leaved evergreens. There is often confusion over when to apply them—before the ground freezes, or after.

There are two reasons for winter mulching: one is to prevent the ground from freezing, or at least to delay it, and the other is to prevent the ground from repeated freeze-thaw cycles, particularly as spring approaches. With new fall plantings and evergreens, the aim is to keep the ground from freezing so that the roots have time to establish and the evergreens can continue to take up water all winter.

For established but tender plants, such as strawberries and some perennials, mulching should be carried out after the ground freezes. A loose mulch of straw, or oak leaves covered over with evergreen boughs, will prevent damaging freeze-thaw cycles and shelter the crowns and roots of plants.

With good growing conditions, plants are more resistant to attack by insects and disease. To increase your insurance, you might want to grow pest and disease resistant or tolerant plants (see Table 13).

✒ Soil Preparation

Knowing what kind of growing conditions you want is easy. Actually achieving them is sometimes difficult, especially with the heavy labour involved in soil preparation. There are various options available, some much easier than others.

In most cases, unless you have a very large area, the top 5 cm of sod should be removed and either buried in the lower levels of soil, or composted. Some people spread a herbicide a week or two earlier to kill deep-rooted perennial weeds and persistent grasses. This is not necessary, but if it is done, make sure that only short-term weed killers are used, such as those containing glyphosate. Residual ones used for driveways and so on will stay in the soil and kill plants for up to six months. In new homes, of course, there is often no vegetation to remove. After this you have four choices, depending on your time, energy, financial resources and soil conditions.

A long term but superb method is to turn chunks of sod upside down in the autumn and leave them to break down over the winter. In the spring, cultivate shallowly several times, ten days apart, to get rid of weeds that grow. Work in lots of organic matter to one spade's depth and then plant buckwheat after all danger of frost is past. When half of it is in flower in the summer, cut it down. Cultivate shallowly several times, and dig in more organic matter, if available. Plant a fall cover crop such as annual rye, and the following spring, dig in more organic matter. The soil is then ready to plant, free of weeds and rich in organic matter.

If you have some reasonably good soil and lots of energy or the resources to hire someone, you can double dig. This will provide soil that is ready to plant in the same season that the sod is first turned. The steps are as follows: remove topsoil to a depth of 15 cm to 20 cm in a narrow trench and store it to one side; break up the lower 15 cm of subsoil with a garden fork or pick axe (you could bury the sod you removed earlier in this deep layer, but break it up first); start another trench beside the first and add this 15 cm to 20 cm of soil to the first trench; work in manure or compost and rotted leaves in this layer (but no sod). Repeat these steps until the entire area is double dug, using the first quantity of soil that was stored to one side to fill in the last trench. Be careful throughout the process not to mix the subsoil and topsoil.

This sort of preparation is good for flower beds, shrub borders, hedges, and vegetable patches. For a large shrub border, where double digging the entire area would be prohibitive, you can double dig wide planting holes for individual shrubs.

If double digging is unreasonable in your circumstances, you can "dig and bring" in the following way: remove rocks and boulders where feasible; turn over and break up the existing soil to a depth of 15 cm to 20 cm, working in rotted leaves and well-rotted manure or compost; and bring in 10 cm to 30 cm of topsoil. Ideally, this last step should be broken into two parts if a large amount of soil is being imported. Bring in half the soil and mix it with the native soil, and then add the remaining soil. If only a thin layer of soil is imported, it should also be mixed with the native soil. The danger in not mixing the two soils is that plants will sometimes grow in the top layer only, with their roots never penetrating deeply into the native soil. This is eventually disastrous for the plants.

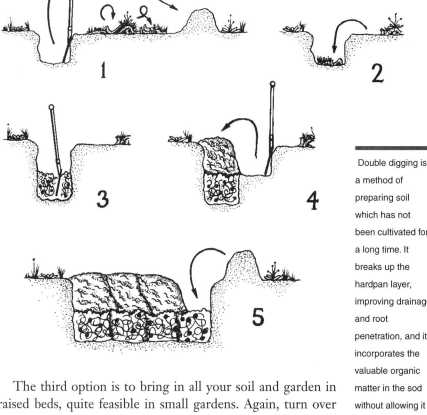

Double digging is a method of preparing soil which has not been cultivated for a long time. It breaks up the hardpan layer, improving drainage and root penetration, and it incorporates the valuable organic matter in the sod without allowing it to regrow. It also enables the gardener to plant in the same season as the ground is broken.

The third option is to bring in all your soil and garden in raised beds, quite feasible in small gardens. Again, turn over and break up the existing soil, if you have any, and then bring in topsoil, mixing in rotted leaves and well-rotted manure or compost. There is no need to edge beds of this depth if the sides are banked, but you can edge with rocks or boards if you want deeper beds or vertical sides.

To determine the amount of topsoil to bring in, first figure out the depth you need. A minimum depth of 15 cm is required for lawns, 20 cm to 30 cm for annual flowers and shallow rooted vegetables, 30 cm to 50 cm for shrubs, shallow-rooted trees, perennial borders, and vegetable plots, and 50 cm to 90 cm for large, deep-rooted trees. Soil is usually purchased in cubic yards, which is 3 feet x 3 feet x 3 feet. One cubic yard, spread to a depth of 4 inches, will cover 9 square yards (7.5 sq metres). One cubic yard, spread to a depth of 12 inches, will cover 3 square yards (3.75 sq metres). The same calculation can be used for estimating shredded bark requirements. Well-rotted manure or compost should be spread to a depth of 2 inches.

Purchased topsoils are often not topsoils at all, so it is wise to work in rotted leaves or other organic matter plus well-rotted manure or compost. You could also grow green manure crops to improve the tilth and fertility of imported or native soils. These are grass or legume crops, often called cover crops because of their use in providing temporary vegetation for bare soils. Plant buckwheat, spring wheat, soybeans or peas in spring and plough the crop under in late summer, then plant annual rye, oats, barley or winter wheat in early autumn and plough them in as soon as the ground can be worked in spring. Alternatively, plant clover or alphalpha in the spring and plough them in the following spring. This is often a good ploy if you have bare soil and haven't had enough time to work out a landscaping plan. Wisely, more jurisdictions are restricting or banning the sale of topsoil. It is possible to create soil, however, and the process is not as slow as one might imagine. Start with clean builders' sand, not beach sand, and work in equal amounts of rotted leaves and compost or manure. In fact, there are many organic materials that can be added, including mushroom compost, rotted hay, old straw, well aged sawdust and seaweed. Existing natural soils should be added as well, so that soil micro-organisms and earthworms can begin their work of creating and improving soil.

✍ Container Planting

Large-scale soil preparation is all very well if you have a large enough garden in which to work, but sometimes you are restricted to growing plants in containers. All the discussion about air, light, nutrient and moisture needs of plants becomes even more important in the difficult growing conditions encountered with the use of containers. The advantages, however, make it worth every effort. It enables gardeners to have trees, shrubs, flowers and vegetables growing on their decks or patios or rooftops to provide screening, wind protection, beauty, fragrance and food. It also makes gardening easier for people who cannot bend down and work at ground level.

Air circulation is often better for plants grown in containers because they are raised above ground level. Air temperature, however, can be quite a problem for container plants because of its effects on soil temperature. During the summer, containers often overheat, and rapid freezing is a problem in winter. Both of these situations are worse in small pots because there is not the buffering effect of large quantities of soil. Large containers used for trees, shrubs and vines should be at least 75 cm high and 100 cm across. Larger is better, but they should not be so tall that they become unstable in wind. Planters used for annual flowers and small vegetables can be as shallow as 20 cm (30 cm is better), but those used for large or root vegetables and perennial flowers should be no less than 30 cm deep, and 50 cm is better. Width should be equal to or greater than the depth, and length can vary from 1 m to 2 m. It is also good practice to move permanent container plants of borderline hardiness into unheated garages or storage areas in winter to prevent freeze-thaw cycles and move very tender specimens into your home over the winter.

There is also a lot of difficulty with lack of air in the root zone because soil compaction is such a problem in container growing. This can be alleviated by mixing in generous quantities of perlite or coarse sand. Vermiculite can be used too. It tends to compress over time, but nutrients do not leach out as quickly. If possible, water from underneath.

Light presents no great problems with container growing. Containers can often be moved around to follow the sun, and this is made easier by installing wheels under large containers, or by putting small pots on a rolling platform.

Steady supplies of nutrients and moisture are difficult to maintain in container plantings because there is no reservoir available. If a container dries out or lacks nutrients, there is nowhere the roots can go in their search. Lots of organic matter will ease the problem, as will the use of mulches. For some reason, gardeners rarely think of mulching the soil in containers, but it is a very effective technique for retaining moisture, preventing overheating in summer and too early a start in spring. Living mulches can be used, too, and any of the small groundcover plants are very attractive. Draping and trailing plants suggested for growing on top of retaining walls can also be used in containers as under-plantings or living mulches. They help to soften and blur the edges of containers or planting boxes and also bring colour, interest and fragrance to a small space. Large containers or planters stay moist longer than small ones, pots in groups lose their moisture more slowly than individual pots, and soil mixes are also slower to dry in plastic pots than in clay. Soil should be moist, never soggy.

Fertilizing can be carried out regularly with a soluble fertilizer, but it is much easier to use slow-release fertilizers mixed into the soil, especially for large plants in containers.

Containers should be at least as wide as they are tall, as life in a small container can be stressful for plants. A large volume of soil makes it easier for the gardener to maintain an even moisture supply and a sufficient nutrient reserve. The containers are also less likely to overheat in the daytime or blow over in the wind.

In constructing planters or large raised beds be sure to make allowance for drainage. Holes of 1.5 cm should be drilled every 15 cm to 20 cm in the bottom of wooden boxes, and the boxes should be set on blocks or legs to allow air to circulate underneath. This will help to lengthen the life of your planters. Raised beds of wood, brick, stone or other materials need larger weep holes near the base. If your raised beds are combined with seating, seats should be 35 cm to 40 cm high and 40 cm to 45 cm wide for most comfortable sitting. Use 1-inch cedar, pressure treated softwood or treat woods with copper naphthanate, a preservative that is nontoxic to plants. Railway ties can also be used, provided they are well-weathered, but it is best to avoid creosoted wood. Large containers containing permanent plantings that will be left outdoors in winter should be insulated inside with below grade insulation. As with every construction project, check the library for ideas and instructions if you are uncertain how to proceed.

In filling your containers, there are various options. For very large containers, you might want to use garden soil

(30%) mixed with compost or rotted leaves (30%) and perlite or coarse sand (40%). Perlite is more expensive but it is also lighter, if weight is a consideration. For large containers and woody plants, use 3 parts shredded bark, 1 part compost and soil, 1 part sand for weight, up to 2 litres lime, and 1 litre 10-10-10 slow release fertilizer per cubic metre. Four litres of well-rotted manure can also be added, if desired. Leave out the lime, though, if you are growing acid-loving plants, and use 50% soil and perlite and 50% coarse peat moss. Packaged mixes are more expensive, but they have the advantage of being weed free and sterile.

Instead of filling large planters with a soil mix, you could fill them with individual pots. This makes it easier to rotate plants throughout the season so that you always have something of interest on display.

If you live in an apartment building, check with the building superintendent before starting a balcony garden. For a roof garden, check the weight restrictions and consider as well the potential problems with shade, wind, and water outlets. Some tips that are helpful for distributing weight on a roof or deck are as follows: set containers on wooden platforms to spread the weight over a larger area; set containers at roof edges, rather than in the middle; use light-weight containers, compressed cellulose or plastic instead of clay or wood; and use light-weight growing mixes.

With careful attention to growing conditions, container plantings can be very successful. So successful, in fact, that plants may outgrow their living quarters. This is not a problem unless woody plants are grown, when moving them on to larger quarters becomes difficult, if not impossible. Root pruning every two to three years is one solution, and this is made easier by using containers with removable sides. Give perennials new growing medium in spring, or replace the top 5 cm to 8 cm in large containers. Even with the best of care container-grown trees, shrubs and vines tend to have shorter lives than they do when grown in the ground. Most of the plants listed in Table 14 are fairly tolerant of drought, although some, such as the broad-leaved evergreens, must be kept evenly moist. It is a good idea to choose pest and disease-resistant plants, since container-grown specimens are already at a disadvantage.

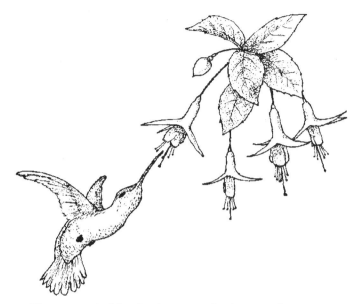

Many gardeners enjoy seeing hummingbirds feeding on the nectar of flowers. These birds are attracted to brightly coloured tubular flowers and may be encouraged to visit even the smallest garden. Fuchsias grown in containers or hanging baskets, for example, are greatly favoured by the little hummingbird. Nectar from flowers is healthier for hummingbirds than the sugar solutions provided by bird lovers in artificial feeders.

Flowers suitable for hanging baskets and containers include:

Achimenes	*Impatiens*	*Schizanthus*
Ageratum	*Ivy-leaved Geranium*	*Strawberry Geranium*
Asparagus Fern	*Lantana*	*Sweet Alyssum*
Browallia	*Lobelia*	*Sweet Pea*
Campanula	*Nasturtium*	*Trailing Petunia*
English Ivy	*Nierembergia*	*Tuberous Begonia*
Fibrous Begonia	*Pansy*	*Vinca minor*
Fuchsia	*Portulaca*	

Erect plants suitable for the middle include:

Bachelor Button	*Dwarf Snapdragon*	*Salvia*
Calendula	*Geranium*	*Verbena*
Carnation	*Marigold*	*Zinnia*
Dianthus	*Nicotiana*	

When growing in containers some thought should be given to their arrangement. In the miniature landscape of a balcony, roof garden or deck, plants are needed at various heights to emphasize the verticality and help to increase the sense of space. That is the value of being able to grow trees, shrubs, and vines in containers. They can even be espaliered.

Scattered, individual pots look lost and out of place, so cluster them instead. Remember to use several heights of vegetation, or place the pots themselves at various levels. If using large containers or planters, plants of varying heights can be grown together in one container. This also reduces the amount of watering needed, because one large container is slower to dry than several small ones. Grouping small ones together, however, will also slow down the rate of drying. If you have an odd assortment of containers, you can tie them together by painting them all one colour. Large heavy containers can be placed on casters or metal pipes so that moving them is easier. The entire look of an outdoor room can be changed by re-arranging the plants.

Although gardening in containers has its challenges, the versatility and the design possibilities they open up is worth every effort.

CHAPTER 7

Themes

Planning a framework for your garden and then choosing plants that will suit the growing conditions builds a sound, functional, attractive garden. You might want to expand this and make your final choice of plants with a theme in mind, one that shows up in some or all of your plants, either in their characteristics or in the function they perform. Some examples would include a fragrance garden, where the lingering memory would be one of wafting scents; an evening garden which features plants that will show up in the gloaming; a rose garden where different varieties of roses are set off with appropriate perennials; an edible garden where many if not all of the plants produce food of some sort; a native garden which uses native or naturalized plants in a naturalistic setting; and a wildlife garden where the structure and plants attract wildlife.

Such themes could encompass the entire garden, if it is not very big, or each room in your garden could have its own theme. Each of these themes will be discussed more fully, and there are others you might want to explore.

Theme gardens reflect the interests of the gardener.

ᔍ Fragrance Garden

For some people, fragrance is synonymous with garden and no landscape would be complete without sweetly scented flowers and foliage. The following shrubs and trees have been arranged according to height, in decreasing order of hardiness, and they would be used as suggested in previous chapters.

Up to 0.6 m
  Garland Flower (Rose Daphne)
  Shrub Roses (R. repens alba, rosea, Henry Hudson, Sea Foam,
    Moje Hammarberg, Nitida Defender, Charles Albanel)
  Lavender, Sage, Rosemary
  Rhododendrum atlanticum-white

Up to 1.2 m

February Daphne
Shrub Roses (Schneezwerg, Kern, Stadt Rosenheim, David
Thompson, Dart's Dash, Cuthbert Grant)
Snowbelle Mock Orange
Mahonia
Burkwood Daphne
Rhododendrum viscosum-white

Up to 2 m

Dwarf Korean Lilac
Bayberry
Shrub Roses (Harison's Yellow, Blanc Double de Coubert, Hansa,
Jens Munk, Therese Bugnet, Pink Surprise, Fred Loads,
Lichtkoenigin Lucia, Agnes, Martin Frobisher)
Mock Orange (Purity and Minnesota)
Butterfly Bush
Azaleas (Carat, Arpege, Daviesi, Jolie Madam,
R. atlanticum, R. luteum, R. roseum)
Korean Spice and Burkwood Viburnums

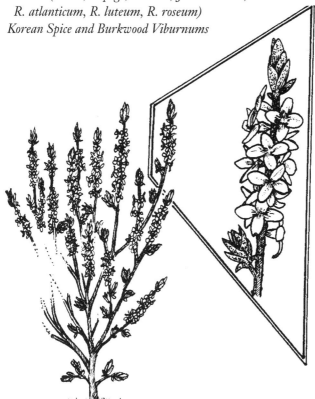

February daphne
(Daphne mezereum) is one of many plants that are fragrant. Locate such plants out of the wind and in places where people sit or pass close by.

Up to 3 m
'Zabelii' Tatarian Honeysuckle
Lilacs
Shrub Roses (William Baffin, Henry Kelsey, John Cabot)
Mock Orange (Sweet, Virginal)
Magnolias (Oyama, Star)
Firethorn
Fragrant Snowball Viburnum

Up to 6 m
Witch Hazel
Russian Olive
Dolgo Crabapple
Nannyberry
Japanese Tree Lilac
Saucer Magnolia
Amur Maple

Up to 15 m or more
American Linden or Basswood
Little Leaf Linden
Balsam Fir
White Cedar
Black Locust

Vines
Hall's Honeysuckle
Wisteria (Chinese, Japanese)
Sweet Autumn Clematis
Jasmine (container)

Foliage plants and flowers of all sorts are also very fragrant, and the following annuals, perennials, bulbs, and tender bulbs are among the best:

Acidanthera	*Daylily*	*Hyacinth*
Artemisia	*Dianthus*	*Iris reticulat*
Basil	*Evening-Scented*	*Lemon Verbena*
Bee Balm	*Stock*	*Lilies—auratum,*
Carnation	*Forget-Me-Not*	*candidum, regale*
Centaurea	*Freesia*	*Lily-of-the-Valley*
Coriander	*Hardy Cyclamen*	*Marjoram*
Daffodil	*Heliotrope*	*Mignonette*

Mint	*Sage*	*Sweet Woodruff*
Narcissus	*Scented Geranium*	*Thyme*
Nicotiana–white	*Sweet Alyssum*	*Tuberose*
Peony	*Sweet Pea*	*Wallflower*
Primrose	*Sweet Violet*	*Valerian*
Rose	*Sweet William*	

Fragrant plants are best used close to where people normally pass or sit. Near doors, windows, around patios and decks, and along walkways are ideal situations. Using them in raised beds or planters brings them even closer to passing noses.

✍ Evening Garden

If a garden is to be used at night, good lighting is essential for safety. It is also helpful in highlighting specimen plants or other garden features and adding depth to a night scene.

The best lighting is unobtrusive. Lights placed under steps or close to the level of walkways do their job without being stark. To light up a large area, several small lights are much more attractive than two or three large floodlights. It is also useful to place these small lights away from the patio so that insects are not brought close. Floodlights, however, can be very effective when used to wash a wall with light or when shone upwards into a tree or large planting. Smaller lights can be used to pick out individual plants or to highlight dark-coloured flowers; red looks particularly striking handled this way. It is also useful to place lights into the nether reaches of the garden. This adds depth to what is otherwise a flat dark mass at night.

There are two methods of wiring a garden. Standard 120-volt wiring must be enclosed and buried about 50 cm underground. It should be installed by an electrician. Low-voltage wiring of 12 volts is connected to a standard power source with a transformer, and can more readily be done by a homeowner. It can be run along the surface of the ground so that you can try out different arrangements before making a final decision and eventually burying the cables. Be sure to do any wiring before outdoor construction, such as a deck, is fully completed.

In the dusk, plants with white flowers stand out particularly well, and there are many from which to choose. If you are short of space, you might want to double up on some themes,

such as white flowered plants for night that are also fragrant.
Fragrant white-flowered plants include:

American Linden	*Lilacs*	*Mock Oranges*
Black Locust	*Little-Leaf Linden*	*Shrub Roses*
Butterfly Bush	*Magnolias*	*Viburnums*

Other plants include, in decreasing order of hardiness,
white flowered forms of:

Up to 0.6 m
> *Heaths and Heathers*
> *Iberis (Evergreen Candytuft)*

Up to 1.2 m
> *Abbotswood Potentilla*
> *Clavey's Dwarf Honeysuckle*
> *Annabelle Hydrangea*

Up to 2 m
> *False Spirea*
> *Dwarf Flowering Crabapples*
> *Garland Spirea*
> *Bristol Snowflake Weigela*
> *Compact Lemoine Deutzia*
> *Azalea*
> *Drooping Leucothoe*
> *Pieris*
> *Rhododendron*
> *Hibiscus*
> *Firethorn*

Up to 3 m
> *Peegee Hydrangea*
> *Elderberry*
> *Enkianthus*
> *Rhododendron*

Up to 6 m
> *Amelanchier*
> *Flowering Crabapples (Dolgo, John Downie, Rescue, Guiding*
> *Star, Snowcloud, White Angel)*
> *Bradford Callery Pear*

Alternate-Leaf Dogwood
Hawthorns (Snowbird, Cockspur)
Cheal's Weeping Cherry
Chinese Flowering Dogwood

Up to 15 m or More
Siberian Pear
Catalpa
European Mountain Ash (Rowan)
Vines
Silver Lace Vine
Sweet Autumn Clematis
Henryi Clematis & other hybrids
Climbing Hydrangea
Wisteria 'Alba'

There are white flowered annuals, perennials, and bulbs as well, including some fragrant ones:

Acidanthera	*Gladiolus*	*Phlox*
Baby's Breath	*Iris*	*Shasta Daisy*
Chrysanthemum	*Narcissus*	*Sweet Alyssum*
Columbine	*Nicotiana*	*Tuberose*
Daffodils	*Petunia*	*Tulips*

As with lights, white-flowered plants that are placed in the more distant parts of the garden will help to add depth to the evening landscape.

✌§ Rose Garden

Roses come in such a wide variety of size, form and colour that they can be used in many ways around the garden. It would be unwise to rely on them entirely to supply all your plant needs, but they can certainly be mixed in freely with other shrubs and flowers, and they can function as ground-covers, barriers, foundation plants, wall plantings, informal hedges, and in shrub borders.

Some flowers seem to go naturally with roses, perhaps because many of them were used several hundred years ago when new roses were being developed, and because of their soft pink, blue and white colours.

Companion plants for roses include:

Artemisia	*Dianthus*	*Lavender*
Aubrieta	*Feverfew*	*Liatris*
Campanula	*Foxglove*	*Lilies, white*
Carnation	*Heuchera*	*Rosemary*
Clematis	*Hollyhock*	*Shasta Daisy*
Columbine	*Iberis*	*Sweet Alyssum*
Cranesbill	*Jacob's Ladder*	*Vinca Minor*
Delphinium	*Iris*	

If you favour yellow and orange roses, you could substitute these colours for the pink companions mentioned above. Blue, mauve, and purple flowers would still be good companions.

A good mix of evergreens, both broad-leaved and coniferous, work well as background for, and intermingled with, roses to provide interest outside of the rose season. The rose season can be extended, of course, by using recurrent or repeat blooming roses. Many hardy shrub roses will continue to bloom right up to the time of heavy frosts and are also very showy with their shiny red hips.

With their wonderful fragrance, broad range of colours and variety in shapes, roses can fill many niches in a garden.

❧ Edible Garden

The plants used to build the structure of an edible garden have the same functions as any other garden: trees producing fruit or nuts can also provide shade, shelter, and screening; fruiting shrubs can be used in hedges, foundation plantings, and shrub borders; fruit trees and bushes can be espaliered; groundcover plants can be chosen for their edibility, and so on. The following lists should illustrate this point.

Suitable nut trees for an edible garden include:

American Beech	*Hazelnut*	*Manchurian Walnut*
Butternut	*Heartnut*	*Swiss Stone Pine*

Fruit bearing trees include:

Amelanchier	*Cherry sweet, sour*	*Nectarine*
Apple	*Cornelian Cherry*	*Peach*
Apricot	*Crabapple*	*Pear*
Black Mulberry	*European Mtn. Ash*	*Plum*

All of these, as well as Currants, Gooseberries and Quince, can be grown as espaliers, either free standing with wire supports, or against a wall or fence.

For screens and windbreaks, use:

Amelanchier	*Highbush Cranberry*	*Siberian Pear*
Cherry	*Nannyberry*	*(pollinator)*
Elderberry	*Plum*	

Fruit trees on dwarf rootstock, genetically dwarfed plants and fruiting shrubs can all be used as hedges in shrub borders, and the smaller ones as foundation plants, and they include:

Amelanchier	*Currants*	*Nectarine*
Apple	*Dwarf Crabapples*	*Peach*
Apricot	*Elderberry*	*Pear*
Beaked Hazelnut	*Gooseberry*	*Plum*
Blueberry	*Mahonia*	*Quince*
Cherry	*Nanking Cherry*	*Shrub Roses*

If you need plants for a barrier, try:

Brambleberries	*Gooseberry*	*Shrub Roses*
Elderberry	*Raspberry*	

Some edible vines, either annual or permanent, include:

Cantaloupe	*Grape Pole Bean*	*Runner Bean*
Cucumber	*Hardy Kiwi*	*Nasturtium*

There are even edible groundcovers:

Chamomile	*Fiddlehead Fern*	*Thyme*
Cranberry	*Strawberry*	*Violet (blue)*
Creeping Mint	*Sweet Woodruff*	

Many vegetables and herbs look attractive on their own or mixed with flowers to form a herbaceous border:

Artichoke	*Chive*	*Parsley*
Basil	*Cucumber*	*Pepper*
Bush Bean	*Eggplant*	*Rhubarb*
Beet	*Endive*	*Rosemary*
Borage	*Fiddlehead Fern*	*Sage*
Cabbage	*Kale*	*Sugar Pea*
Cantaloupe	*Leek*	*Summer Squash*
Chard	*Okra*	

There are also some edible flower petals, or their leaves. Here are a few:

Beebalm	*Johnny-Jump-Up*	*Nasturtium*
Calendula	*Lemon Verbena*	*Pelargonium*
Chrysanthemum	*Marigold*	*Rose*
Impatiens	*Daylily (buds)*	*Sage*

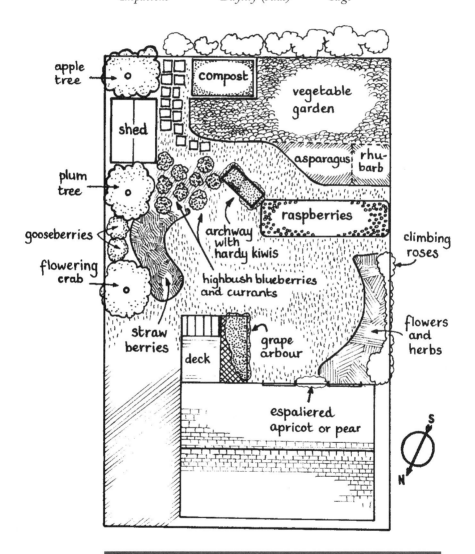

Edible plants can be used to create a garden that is both functional and attractive. Use fruit trees as screens and windbreaks; fruiting shrubs (e.g. blueberries) and perennial vegetables (asparagus and rhubarb) to define boundaries and provide enclosure; and low growing fruits as ground covers.

Edible landscaping is a fairly straightforward exercise. Most of the plants thrive in full sun, and some of the shrubs and trees require two varieties for proper pollination and fruit or nut production. If you have an old apple tree that needs rejuvenation, or want to know more about fruiting shrubs and trees, Bart Hall-Beyer and Jean Richard give excellent information in their book *Ecological Fruit Production in the North*, (1983, published by authors, Trois-Rivieres, Que.).

Some garden plants are poisonous, and these should be avoided where small children play. They include the berries, flowers, leaves, seeds, roots or bulbs of:

Azalea	*Delphinium*	*Larkspur*
Black Locust	*Elderberry, raw*	*Morning Glory*
Bleeding Heart	*English ivy*	*Narcissus*
Castor Bean	*Foxglove*	*Oak*
Choke Cherry	*Holly*	*Privet*
Crocus	*Honeysuckle*	*Rhododendron*
Daffodil	*Hyacinth*	*Wisteria*
Daphne	*Iris*	*Yew*

If you suspect that someone has ingested parts of any of these plants, call your physician or poison control centre immediately. Tell them the name of the plant and what parts were eaten, how much and when, the age of the person, and any symptoms you have noticed.

✌§ Native Garden

The use of native materials and natural landscaping appeals for several reasons. This theme fits in more readily with gardens backing onto wilderness or untamed land. A native garden requires much less maintenance than traditional gardens, it helps to preserve plants that might otherwise be erased by bulldozers, and it makes use of the basic structure and features of the site. It also reduces or eliminates the need for fertilizers, mowing, herbicides and pesticides, in part because of the natural resistance of native materials to pests and diseases.

You might decide to naturalize just one corner of your garden, as under a mature tree, choosing plants that would be found in that tree's understory; you might choose to naturalize your entire garden or cottage plot; or you might want to ease a traditional landscape into a neighbouring wilderness, as discussed in Chapter 5.

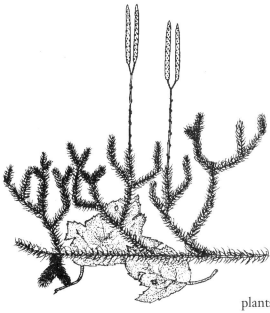

Plants tend to form natural groupings or communities. Forest communities, for example, are composed of large canopy trees, perhaps some understory trees, another layer of small trees and shrubs and a ground layer of herbaceous plants. An exposed coastal area would have only a few small shrubs and an extensive ground layer. A meadow is another natural community of only one layer, although shrubs and trees are always encroaching at the edges. You could use only plants that are found in your area, or you could select plants that are found together naturally but far away geographically. The important thing is to match plants with similar needs in climate, light, nutrients, moisture and shelter.

Club moss *(Lycopodium clavatum)* is one of many native plants that form the ground cover layer in open woodlands, sometimes covering the ground thickly. Keeping woodland or other native plants is a good way of remembering the past heritage of the site of your garden.

Diekelmann and Schuster have excellent plant lists in their book *Natural Landscaping. Designing with Native Plant Communities* (McGraw Hill, 1982). An example of a natural community would be a Chestnut and Oak forest, with Red Maple and Red Oak as dominant trees, Striped Maple, Green Ash, Butternut and Amelanchier as understory trees, shrubs of Witch Hazel, Mountain Laurel, Rhododendron and Azalea and a ground layer of Wintergreen, Christmas Fern, Wild Sarsaparilla and False Solomon's Seal. Some of these are plainly not native, and Chestnut has disappeared, but they do form a natural community and provide a way of incorporating Mountain Laurel, Rhododendron and Azalea into a naturalistic setting. A forest dominated by Hemlock would also have these three shrubs but would have a slightly different mix with a more boreal component in the ground layer. That is, there would be Wild Lily-of-the-Valley, Clintonia (Bluebead Lily), Club-Mosses, Partridgeberry, Foamflower, Trillium and Star-Flower.

Much of the northeast is covered in boreal forest, with its Balsam Fir, White and Red Spruce. The understory includes

Striped and Mountain Maple, Birches, Red, Jack and White Pines, Aspens, Pin Cherry, Red Oak and American Mountain Ash. The shrub layer in it contains Amelanchier, Beaked Hazelnut, Mountain Holly, Canada Yew, Hobblebush, Witherod, Bayberry and Common Juniper, and the ground layer is composed of the well known forest floor flowers Trailing Arbutus (Mayflower), Bluebead Lily, Bunchberry, Twinflower, Painted Trillium, Wild Lily-of-the-Valley, Mosses, Ferns and berry plants (Black Crowberry, Foxberry, Partridgeberry, Huckleberry and Wild Blueberry). An exposed coastal area would have many of the same berry plants as well as Dwarf Birches, Rhodora (Wild Rhododendron), Bearberry, and Bayberry. Spruce woods and pine forests would have a different mix of plants, although many would be duplicates of the boreal forest. A bog is another natural community, and the northeast abounds with them.

To create a woodland, you can either start with mature trees and replace the lawn underneath with shrubs and ground layer plants, or you can start with a weed-free seed bed and plant young fast growing trees, gradually replacing and filling in with slower trees and understory plants. Whenever possible, rescue plants from land that is going to be developed, or propagate herbaceous plants with seeds or cuttings. Transplanting trees from the wild is discussed in Chapter 2. If transplanting herbaceous plants, dig a very wide circle when lifting the plant in order to provide it with a large volume of its native soil. This will give it more time to adjust before it has to grow its roots into the new soil.

If you want to create a meadow, there are several options:

1 • In a sunny area, start with a weed-free seedbed and plant with appropriate seeds you have collected. Purchased wildflower seeds tend to contain many annuals, but you might want to try them.

Large cranberries (*Vaccinium macrocarpon*) thrive in bogs and wetlands. If you want some in the garden, leave a natural site undisturbed and develop the garden around this piece of natural heritage.

2 • Dig small patches in an existing lawn, set in plants or seeds, and surround with shingles or newspapers to prevent competition until the new plants are well established. Bare soil invites undesirable weeds.

3 • Rake hard on a small lawn area or use a dethatcher to loosen turf, and then sprinkle seeds over the area. Scratch in gently with a rake. Again, use seeds you have collected yourself, and plant them when they normally drop from the plant. Avoid Chicory, Queen Anne's Lace and Evening Primrose if you can, and be vigilant in weeding the first two or three years.

In all cases, a poor infertile soil is best so that the grasses don't out compete the flowers. To reduce fertility in an established lawn, mow for several seasons, removing the grass clippings, and do not fertilize.

To prevent the meadow looking untidy, keep lawn areas and grass paths well cut and trimmmed so that the meadow looks as if it were intentional.

The mowing pattern you use in your meadow (for you will have to do a bit of mowing) will determine the kinds of flowers that survive and flower. Mowing from July onwards encourages spring flowering plants; mowing until June, and then again in mid September, encourages the summer flowering plants; and doing no mowing until late September produces autumn flowering plants, as long as the cuttings are removed. Seed will reproduce from the flowers left unmowed.

To create a bog or wetland, see Chapter 8. Use native plants to fill it, being careful to avoid weedy species. If you have a natural wet spot, remove the existing vegetation and then plant it to natives. In the centre pool, where water is deepest, you might choose White or Yellow Water Lilies. Where it is shallower but still distinctly wet, you could try Water Arum (Wild Calla), Sedge and Large and Small Cranberries. Where it is slightly drier, the natural plants would be Bog Rosemary, Sedges, Blue Flag, Pitcher Plant and Cranberries. The moss heath at the very edges could include Leatherleaf, Bog Rosemary, Swamp (Bog) Laurel, Labrador Tea, Cranberries, Chokeberry, Huckleberry, Mountain Holly, Sphagnum Moss, Swamp (Bog) and Dwarf Birches, Bayberry and Rhodora.

If you have a naturally swampy area and want to introduce some natural plants, set them in and then surround them with a mulch, or use wooden shingles to prevent competition, until the introduced plants are well established.

✦ Wildlife Garden

Attracting wildlife to a garden often goes hand in hand with natural landscaping because of the appeal of native plants to wildlife, but many non-native plants are also very effective. Providing the basic needs of shelter, food and water draws the wildlife, and knowing the needs of the particular visitors you hope to attract is half the battle.

The forms of shelter and the types of food and drink vary for different creatures. A pond which may be shelter for some species is a source of drinking water for others; the shrubs that provide berries for birds also provide shelter for birds and other small animals; the butterflies so carefully planted for become food for resident birds; the butterfly bush that is a source of nectar for butterflies is also a hunting ground of hummingbirds for tiny spiders and insects; and so on. A gardener could focus on creating a specialized area, such as a butterfly or hummingbird garden, but wildlife does not occur in isolation. A rich variety in the landscape is more likely to attract a diversity of wildlife, and there is a greater chance of having one or another creature visible on any day for the gardener to observe and enjoy. The particular attractions for some wildlife, however, will be noted throughout.

Shelter can be anything from a pile of rocks for reptiles and invertebrates to a woodland edge for birds and small mammals. The key is to have variety. Birds like edges, and a mixed shrub planting between a background of trees and an open, sunny area accomplishes this. Several layers, or a variety in heights, and a mixture of deciduous and evergreen plants is best. Different birds use different layers, and they prefer different plants for food and shelter. This edge can be enriched with piles of logs, brush piles, rock piles and decay in the form of leaf mould, shredded bark and rotting logs, to appeal to a wide variety of small animals. Toads, for example, which are wonders at eating insects, like a cool damp place to which they can retire, and a pile of logs or rocks suits them perfectly. The volume of this edge can be increased by planting in generous curves rather than regimented lines.

Following is a list of shrubs and trees suitable for a wildlife planting, including plants noted for the cover they provide or for the food they produce in the form of pollen, nectar, berries and nuts for a wide variety of animals. They are arranged according to height in roughly decreasing order of hardiness.

There are several native viburnums that produce berries attractive to wildlife. Viburnums are vigorous plants with attractive leaves and panicles of flowers.

Up to 0.6 m

February Daphne	*Cotoneasters*
Shrub Roses	*Heaths, Heathers*

Up to 1.2 m

Pygmy Caragana	*Shrub Roses*
Currants	*Japanese Quince*
Raspberries	*Mahonia*
Brambles	*Azaleas*

Up to 2 m

Cotoneasters	*Azaleas*
Red Osier Dogwood	*Burning Bush*
Bayberry	*Flowering Quince*
Dwarf Crabapples	*Viburnums*
Shrub Roses	*Butterfly Bush*
Blueberry	*Firethorn*
Weigelas	*Hibiscus*
Willows	

Up to 3m

Caragana	*Winterberry*
Cotoneasters	*Viburnums*
Honeysuckle	*Purple-Leaf Sandcherry*
Lilacs	*Privets*
Amelanchier	*Beauty Bush*
Elderberry	*Cornelian Cherry*

Up to 6 m

Caragana	*Pussy Willow*
Choke Cherry	*Crabapples*
Nannyberry	*Alternate-Leaf Dogwood*
Amelanchier	*Hawthorns*
Black Mulberry	*Cornelian Cherry*
Purple-Leaf Sandcherry	*Chinese Flowering Dogwood*

Up to 15 m or more
    Spruces   *Maples*
    Pines   *Oaks*
    Birches   *Beech*
    European Mountain Ash   *Nut Trees*

Vines
    Honeysuckles   *Trumpet Vine*
    Grape   *Wintercreeper*
    Bittersweet   *Baltic Ivy*

As well as forming edges between woods and open areas, these plants can function as hedges, windbreaks, screens, and in shrub borders in traditional landscapes.

If a mixed border of shrubs and trees is not possible, a hedge can do a fine job of providing dense cover and nesting sites, and all your shrub and tree trimmings piled underneath the hedge can provide additional shelter for other small animals. A mixed hedge of deciduous shrubs is preferred, using suggestions from above, and conifers are good mixed in. Perhaps there is room for only a few vines; they too can provide food and shelter.

In creating a good edge, you have probably also created an open, sunny, sheltered area that is heaven to butterflies. They also like warm rocks, logs and other roosts, and every effort must be made to shelter them from breezes. Rocky outcrops and a variety of slopes will add interest and will also help to provide little pockets of shelter for butterflies and other creatures.

Your yard cannot be treated in isolation when considering the proportion of cover and open areas. If you live in a grove of trees, you might want to open up a glade in your little forest. Edge areas could be created by planting shrubs around such open areas as patio, driveway, walkways and any bit of lawn you have. These shrubs should be of different heights to create more layers. If you live in a very open area, on the other hand, you might want to plant trees and break up large expanses with patches of shrubs. A single mature tree can be vastly improved for shelter by underplanting with a variety of shrubs. You could have a fairly thick foundation planting with open areas close to the house for bird feeders and bird baths, and flower borders for butterflies.

If you can possibly arrange it, a pond is an absolute must for attracting wildlife. Frogs and toads and an array of insects will be right at home there, and birds and small animals might visit. A pond can also be used as a focal point for the garden, but if your summers are particularly humid and hot, you might prefer to do without one because evaporation worsens the situation. Chapter 8 discusses location and building of ponds and wetlands.

Water can also be provided in other ways. A little fountain spraying water over a rocky puddle is safe for toddlers and provides ready moisture for animals. Small insects such as moths and butterflies need moisture rather than open water, and a boggy patch is quite suitable. Birds will make active use of a bird bath if it is properly situated. It should be at least 1m high if it is in the open, and a distance of 2 m to 3 m away from shrubbery will give birds ready access to cover, if needed. Keep it hosed off and refilled daily, especially in summer.

As well as shelter and water, wildlife need food, not just at the height of summer but from early spring to late fall, and into winter for some creatures. Much of this can be provided by the plants used in landscaping. That open sunny sheltered area for butterflies would provide lots of nectar if it were a wildflower meadow, or if it were bordered by a generous riot of flowers. Butterflies need a variety of colourful, fragrant flowers that extend from early spring through to late fall, and hummingbirds seem to favour bright red, pink and orange tubular flowers. Many of the plants in the following list are favoured by butterflies, bees and birds for their nectar, pollen, or seeds, and an informal flower border near the house brings visitors into view from the windows.

Birds are attracted to seed heads of wildflowers and garden plants.

Ageratum	*Corabells*	*Jacob's Ladder*	*Scabiosa*
Ajuga	*Cosmos*	*Jewelweed*	*Scarlet Runner*
Alyssum	*Cranesbill*	*Liatris*	*Shasta Daisy*
Arabis	*Dahlia*	*Lilies*	*Showy Sedum*
Aster	*Doronicum*	*Michaelmas Daisy*	*Snapdragon*
Aubrieta	*Fireweed*	*Nasturtium*	*Sunflower*
Bee Balm	*Foxglove*	*Oenothera*	*Sweet Alyssum*
Bleeding Heart	*Fuchsia*	*Oriental Poppy*	*Sweet William*

Butterfly Weed	*Gaillardia*	*Petunia*	*Verbena*
Calendula	*Globeflower*	*Phlox (Moss Pink)*	*Veronica*
California Poppy	*Goldenrod*	*Rudbeckia*	*Wallflower*
Cardinal Flower	*Heliotrope*	*Sage*	*Yarrow*
Centaurea	*Iberis*	*Salvia*	*Zinnia*
Chrysanthemum			

Shrubs are important, too, and early flowering ones such as pussy willows and spring blooming heaths (King George, Springwood Pink, Arthur Johnson, Cherry Stevens and Darley Dale) are particularly important food sources to early emerging butterflies. February Daphne is also useful, and *Cotoneaster adpressus* will attract Red Admirals. Butterfly Bush, of course, is invaluable for attracting butterflies, especially the *Nymphalidae*. The list of shrubs and trees on pages 121 to 122 includes other shrubs that are valuable as sources of nectar and pollen for butterflies, hummingbirds and bees.

Butterflies, bless their little hearts, also have a larval stage which devours foliage of sometimes desirable plants. A familiar example is the Cabbage White, but it is not generally a big problem. Birds will eat butterflies and their larvae, but they also eat a host of lawn and garden pests. If you want butterflies but not the birds, avoid berried shrubs. If you want to do more for the birds than provide berried shrubs, you might want to consider bird feeders. These are best located in the open in view of a window, and about 2 m or 3 m from trees or shrubs for quick escape from predators if necessary. They could be chest or head-high, and a metal cone on the post will inhibit attack by cats. Encouraging neighbours to put bells around their cats' necks will also help to protect birds from them. A mixture of seeds, corn and fat (not bread) has wide appeal, and a commitment is needed to keep feeders well stocked, especially in winter.

Themes of fragrance, evening, roses, edibility, native plants and wildlife are just some examples of possible themes for a garden. Others might include colour or shape or herbs. A theme should reflect the interests of the gardener; someone with a large area could indulge themselves with different themes for different areas. It depends on what you have to work with and what you like.

CHAPTER 8

Features

F eatures in the garden are rather like furnishings in a house. The garden can exist without them, but features add interest and give focus to various rooms in the garden. As discussed in Chapter 1, a feature in direct relationship with a door or window forms a focal point, and a garden can be built up around this line of vision. A feature might also be placed near the intersection of two paths, or next to an entrance. In large gardens there would be space for several features, such as a rockery, peat garden, water in some form, garden seat, ancient tree, pergola and others. Small gardens would be more restricted, but even a tiny patio or balcony can have a feature. It would, of course, be small enough to match the scale and might be a single potted plant, a fountain, or an attractive statue.

Features add interest and give focus to various rooms in the garden.

Water

Water is perhaps the most commanding feature and can range in size from a bowl of water to a large pond. Looking at or listening to water tends to make one feel cooler and lends an air of tranquility. Water also presents an opportunity to grow certain plants and in the right position can attract wildlife. The disadvantages are that it can make a muggy site feel even worse, and it could be a danger to toddlers.

If you are using containers for your water, a 110-litre (25-gallon) size or more is good, and it should be leakproof. A half barrel would be suitable, or a cluster of several, but smaller containers are also acceptable if that is all you have room for. The smaller the container, though, the greater the temperature fluctuations.

Whatever you use should get plenty of sunshine. Place it in view of a window, in the centre of a group of shrubs or flowers, near a path intersection, or anywhere else it can be readily seen. A small reflecting bowl, for example, would look very attractive next to a seat or garden bench. Containers can be sunk into the ground, but for anything of appreciable size it is probably wiser to dig a hole.

To create a bog, wetland, or pond, you have two choices. If you already have a wet patch, you can use it for a bog or wetland, clearing the existing vegetation and planting it with a variety of plants. Do not position a pond with a liner there because the digging is very difficult, and ground water will push up the liner from underneath. The other choice is to create a bog or dig a pond in a dry area, using a liner to conserve moisture. Position a pond where it will receive plenty of sunshine to encourage a greater variety of insect and animal life. Avoid overhanging trees if possible because of the risk of root damage and the considerable leaf drop in autumn. Place a pond on the lower part of a slope, which seems more realistic, and if you have a natural wetland, you could position the pond above to overflow into the wetland. A natural stream could be dammed to create a pond, and you would have the benefit of the sound of running water. If you want it near the house, place it where it can be readily seen and make it a garden feature. You might even be able to use rainwater from the gutter run off to keep it replenished. If you are creating a wetland as well, position it behind or to the side of the pond where it can be seen more readily. The soil you remove in digging the pond can be used to build a sloping rockery or display garden of treasured plants.

To make the pond, use a butyl rubber lining or heavy, flexible polythene. Roofing membrane, a rubber product available in 30 to 40 ml thickness, can be purchased from roofing suppliers. Reinforced polyvinyl chloride does not last as long, and polyethylene lasts only a year or two. Concrete cracks too readily, and preformed fibreglass ponds are too steep sided and usually too small.

Dig a saucer-shaped hollow; an area 1.2 m by 1.5 m is adequate, but an area twice as large will keep water temperatures from fluctuating madly. Dig lots of shallow edge or shelf, about 25 cm deep by 25 cm wide, for a wide variety of plant life. The edge can be quite extensive if you want a bog as well. Make sure that the edge is the same level all the way around the pond so that no liner shows when filled with water. Make it at least 60 cm deep in the middle, and then dig an extra 15 cm deep over the entire area.

Remove all sharp stones and spread the area with 5 cm of damp sand. This acts as a protective cushion for the liner. Lay the liner over the hole with the centre barely touching the middle, and weight the edges with heavy stones. In the boggy end, if you have one, slit holes for drainage. Add a 4 cm layer of sand and then 6 cm to 10 cm subsoil, but use a mixture of soil and plenty of peat moss in the boggy end. Gradually fill with water by laying the end of a hose on a board. Fill slowly and gently, letting the water press the rubber into the contours, and smooth out any wrinkles. Trim the edges so that there remains a flap of liner lying over the edge of the hole, and finish the edge of the pool with more soil or rocks to anchor the liner edges.

Let your pond stand for a week or more before planting. You can start in late spring or early summer, when the water is warm enough that you can get into it without freezing your feet. To plant it, use vegetation that is suited to deep, intermediate and shallow depths. The variety of plants increases as the depth decreases, which is why a lot of shallow water around the edge is a good idea. Hardy plants can be planted directly into the soil lining the pond, but tender plants can be anchored container and all in the pond soil. Tender plants are usually treated as annuals, but they can be removed from the pond each autumn and overwintered in non-freezing water.

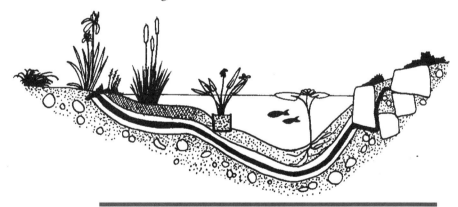

Ponds with a wide, shallow edge create growing conditions for a variety of plants that require wetness. Here, an impermeable layer has been laid at the bottom of an excavation. One side of the pond is layered with large stones, some of which anchor the impermeable layer. Containers can be used to grow tender aquatic plants, making them easier to remove in the autumn, but hardy plants can root in the shallow mud at the bottom of the pond. Here flags line the pond, there are cattails in the shallow water and lilies are rooted in the deeper water. Plants in ponds require annual thinning if open water is to be retained.

Once the plants are in, you could add snails and goldfish to help keep the pool clean. Fish will need wintering indoors as well, unless the water is more than 60cm deep. A pail of mud and pond water will get the insect life off to a good start, as well as an algal bloom, or you can wait for the insects to find it themselves (blackflies will most certainly locate it). Add frog and toad spawn rather than adult animals because of the homing instinct of these amphibians.

In the centre of the pool, Water Lilies are a good choice and can be purchased as plants or grown from seed. Lots of sunshine means more blooms, provided the water is warm and quiet, and the shade their leaves provide reduces the amount of green algae. Water Lilies come as large, medium, small, and pygmy sizes and in shades of red, pink, white and yellow. Thus there are plants for even the smallest tub or pool, because Water Lilies need water depths that match their sizes. You could also plant Arrow-head and Horsetail for a natural look.

Along the shelf where the marginal plants grow, there is a choice of:

Arrowhead
Aquatic Forget-me-Not
Blue Flag
Calamus (Sweet Flag)
Cotton Grass
Golden Button

Manna Grass
Marsh Marigold
Monkeyflower
Water Plantain
Yellow Iris

Creating wet areas encourages frogs and other wildlife that require wet conditions, and they help to keep the garden free of flies.

Several of these are plants native to or naturalized in the northeast.

Hornwort is an oxygenating plant that can be used, but you might want to stay away from the weedy oxygenators Elodea and Pondweed. Fountains will help to aerate a pond; just be sure to use a pump with enough power to lift the volume of water you need to the height you want. Along the very edges of the pond and in the boggy part, or if you simply have a natural boggy patch, there is a tremendous variety of native and cultivated plants that can be used:

Aruncus	*Joe-Pye-Weed*
Astilbe	*Meadowsweet*
Beebalm	*Mint*
Calla Lily	*Monkeyflower*
Camassia	*Monkshood*
Cardinal Flower	*Ornamental Rhubarb*
Crested Iris	*Primula*
Fringed Loosestrife	*Siberian Iris*
Fringed Orchid	*Swamp Milkweed*
Globeflower	*Swamp Rose Mallow*
Hosta	*Turtlehead*
Jack-in-the-Pulpit	*Virginia Bluebell*
Japanese Iris	

These plants would also be suitable for use along stream banks and edges of lakes. Suitable ferns for damp positions would include Cinnamon Fern, Maidenhair Fern, Male Fern and Royal Fern. Lady Fern also grows in damp positions but is too invasive for most gardens. Table 12 lists shrubs and trees that will grow in wet conditions. Water is a delightful feature for any garden and greatly expands the kinds of plants that can be grown. Even a problematic wet patch in a garden can be turned into a definite asset with a planting of water-tolerant plants.

✌§ Specimen Plants

Specimen plants are often used as features. They may be huge and impressive, such as a stately old tree, or much smaller, such as a shrub with characteristics that appeal in several seasons, or small and contained, such as a handsome plant in an attractive pot or tub. The size would depend in part on the size of the garden and the size of the particular room it is in.

A garden can have several specimen plants, but be selective. If too many specimens are used, they become distracting.

Some places they might be used are in the centre front of a shrub border, outside a window, or beside an entry. Try not to place them close to another feature. If a pond, for example, has first priority as a feature in your garden, do not put a particularly striking plant right next to it, or they will compete for attention. To accentuate a specimen tree or shrub, underplant it with spring bulbs and summer flowers.

In choosing specimen plants, look for those with a striking shape or unusual colouring or attractive foliage or whatever appeals to you. Those that have some characteristic of interest in each season of the year, even in winter if visible from the house, would be good choices. They might have an attractive winter outline or be evergreen, produce flowers or coloured foliage in spring, bloom in summer or have unusually coloured leaves, and turn colour in autumn or be covered in berries. Most importantly, however, they must be attractive and appealing to you.

✌§ Rockeries

Rockeries are probably the most labour-intensive feature of any garden. They require heavy work to build and take many hours of maintenance once completed, so only the most committed of gardeners should attempt them. Natural rock gardens are slightly easier to deal with because they are already built. They would include natural rock outcroppings, peat beds, solid ledges and cliffs, woodlands, rocky meadows, and broken rock or scree. Those that are large enough to rely on shrubs as well as a few perennials are also easier to maintain than those planted entirely with herbaceous perennials.

Peat beds and rocky meadows or boulder gardens are more suited to the coastal conditions of eastern Canada and will be used as examples in the following discussion.

Boulder gardens tend to have damp patches mixed in with generally well drained areas and are usually quite sunny. The plants in the following lists, in decreasing order of hardiness, would be suitable for boulder gardens and also for rock outcroppings if good sized pockets of soil were available. The broad-leaved evergreens, Daphnes, Heaths and Heathers, and Japanese Maple are best placed in the damp areas, or not used at all if conditions are very dry. The following plants are grouped according to height in decreasing order of hardiness.

A rock garden using existing boulders and outcrops and planted with small shrubs and a few perennials is easier to create and maintain than rock gardens using imported rocks and only perennials. Attractive small native trees, such as Indian Pear *(Amelanchier)*, do well under these conditions, and the garden can have the added interest of carpets of mosses and lichens.

Deciduous Shrubs Under 0.6 m

Dyer's Greenwood
Genista species
Bean's Broom
Spirea 'Little Princess,' 'Bullata'
Cotoneasters

Lavender
Rock Rose (Helianthemum)
Purple Broom
St. John's Wort
Spanish Gorse

Evergreen Shrubs Under 0.6 m

Bearberry
Huckleberry
Cliff Green
Vinca minor (Periwinkle)
Azaleas
Heath, Heather

Cotoneasters
Small Leaved Rhododendrons
Iberis (Evergreen Candytuft)
Pincushion Box
Garland Flower (Rose Daphne)

Mixed Shrubs to 1.2 m or more

Pygmy Caragana
Anthony Waterer Spirea
February Daphne
Potentilla (Cinquefoil)
Dwarf Birch
Troost Birch
Shrub Roses

Dwarf Korean Lilac
Golden Mock Orange
Azaleas
Rhododendrons
Burkwood Daphne
Cutleaf Purple Japanese Maple

The larger shrubs, of course, would be suitable only for larger rock gardens. Dwarf and small conifers would be an excellent asset, either as accent points or to create backgrounds. Microbiota is a lovely, small evergreen, and there are dwarf varieties of Balsam Fir, False Cypress, Hemlock, Spruce, Cedar *(Thuja)*, Yew, Juniper and Pine. The last three kinds are most tolerant of dry conditions, once established, but save the others for moist areas.

Suitable bulbs would include: Anemone, Chiondoxa, Hardy Cyclamen, Eranthus, small Iris, Daffodils and Tulips, both hybrids and species, Grape Hyacinth, and Narcissus.

If a rock garden does not seem complete to you without a few perennials, the following list might help fill in the small, sunny nooks and crannies:

Alyssum	*Columbine*	*Saxifrage*
Arabis	*Dianthus*	*Sedum*
Arenaria	*Draba*	*Sempervivum*
Aubrieta	*Iberis*	*Thrift (Armeria)*
Basket-of-Gold	*Phlox (Moss Pink)*	*Thyme, creeping*
Campanula	*Potentilla*	*Veronica*
Creeping Baby's Breath		*Woolly Yarrow*

Many of these perennials and bulbs are suitable for growing in planted dry walls, and you could satisfy an urge for rock gardening with a planted wall (see Chapter 3). They would also be suitable for planting in rock faces wherever suitable pockets of soil could be located.

For a rock garden peat bed conditions have to be moist, and the soil has to be acidic, well drained and built up with generous quantities of peat moss. These conditions occur naturally in Atlantic Canada. The larger plants for the most part need shelter from winter winds. Most of the plants in the following list are Ericaceous, so that Rhododendrons, for example, are closely related to Lambkill, Blueberries, and Pieris. Those marked * are edible native plants of the northeast.

Shrubs Under 0.6 m

Bearberry	*Cranberries*	*Lambkill*
Black Crowberry	*Foxberry*	*Mountain Heath*
Blueberries	*Heaths, Heathers*	*Partridge Berry*
Bog Rosemary	*Huckleberry*	*Rhodora*
Bunchberry	*Labrador Tea*	*Small-Leaved Rhododendrons*

Shrubs Up to 1.2 m or more

Azaleas	**Highbush Blueberry*	*Mountain Laurel*
Bog Birch	*Leatherleaf*	*Pieris*
Enkianthus	*Leucothoe*	*Rhododendrons*

Most of the native plants transplant poorly from the wild but they may be propagated using soil layering, cuttings, or seed. They will also have more attractive shapes when home propagated and given plenty of room to grow. Bog Rosemary, for example, usually looks thin and lanky when competing in the wild with other plants, but grown from cuttings with lots of space it forms a most attractive, spreading plant.

Many of these plants do well in partial shade with sun in the morning. Where summers are particularly warm, the high overhead shade provided by tall trees may be required all day, or at least during the hottest part of the day. Heaths and Heathers, however, need maximum sunlight, so do not crowd them with other plants. They look best planted in groups of three or more, and they are available in a wide variety of foliage and flower colour with blooming times from spring through to autumn. Again, a mix of small and dwarf evergreens, particularly the moisture-loving ones, will do well as background or accent plants.

If you want a few perennials, you might find some in the following list that appeal to you:

Astilbe	*Fringed Bleeding Heart*	*Lilies*
Bloodroot	*Garden Phlox*	*Primulas*
Columbine	*Hardy Cyclamen*	*Saxifrage*
Foamflower	*Jacob's Ladder*	*Trillium*

Moisture-loving ferns for the peat bed would include Maidenhair, Rock Polypody, Green and Maidenhair Spleenworts and Royal Fern. Avoid the invasive Sensitive Fern unless you want a large area filled in.

It should be emphasized that rock gardens built from scratch and relying heavily on perennials are far more work than those using natural rockeries and shrubby plants.

❧ Seating

Many gardens are designed as tranquil oases to wander and perhaps sit down and ponder. For this reason, comfortable, well placed seating is a great addition to any garden. The best seat spots are open to sun with some shelter from chilling breezes. A seat next to the shelter of a large, warm, sunny boulder or in the shelter of a rocky outcrop would be a good use for difficult rocks. If your garden tends to overheat for more than a week or two in summer, you might prefer, instead, to place a seat where it catches little, cooling puffs of air. Deep shade is not a good idea, because seats in that position tend not to be used at all, even on the hottest of days.

Unless you want a completely secluded seat, it should also face areas of activity, of either humans or wildlife. A bench near the children's play area, next to a pond, in view of a bird feeder, overlooking the road or sidewalk, are all close to places of action without intruding on them. You might also want a quiet peaceful seat near a rose or fragrance garden or overlooking a fine view. There is often room for more than one seat in a garden.

The seat should also be comfortable, with a generous planting nearby to give some sense of enclosure. It could also be placed in a shelter of some sort, such as a painted trellis gazebo in a more formal garden or a rustic gazebo built of raw timbers and twigs in a naturalistic setting. This helps to create filtered light around the seat, which is somehow very satisfying to the human psyche. The filtered light could also be created with a small tree nearby, or with vines tumbling over a lattice or frame. The seat itself should match the surroundings, ranging from wrought iron and wicker through to unpainted wooden benches and seats carved from logs.

The considerations just discussed are the most important in locating seats. It might work out that you could also make the seat a focal point from a window or door. It is so inviting to look out and see a bench waiting for you to step into the garden and sit a while on it.

✌ Ornaments

Ornaments come in a wide variety of shapes and sizes and, if used tastefully, add to a garden's charm. They can be large or small, formal or informal, whimsical or stately, depending on your taste and garden. Some might improve with age and weathering, and others might be better stored indoors each winter. They can also act as transition elements, taking a little of the indoors out to the garden.

A plant in an attractive pot or container might be just the ticket for that bare spot by your back steps. Maybe you have always fancied a sundial but never got around to finding one. Perhaps your sense of humour calls for a clay toad nestled in the flower bed. These are just a few examples of garden ornaments. Pink flamingos and painted butterflies might not be to your taste, but there are lots of other ornaments that probably would appeal to you, and they add a touch of beauty, humour, and surprise to any garden.

A difficult situation can be turned into a feature. Some of the rocky features in this garden, created within an old quarry, have been hidden and others have been enhanced. Here, a garden seat nestles out of the wind in the shelter of a warm, rocky outcrop.

✨ Unwanted Features

Features can be created by enhancing natural features, such as boulders or boggy corners, or by adding man made elements attractively—a wooden bench or sundial. What about eyesores, though, in feature positions?

Tree stumps, old wells and large granite rocks are not easily moved, and the only solution is to enhance or hide them. Surrounding them with flowers and shrubs might help to blend them into the garden, or it might draw unwanted attention to them. Each situation has to be carefully assessed. Vines, of course, are a good solution for hiding eyesores. They don't even have to grow very densely, but they must be attractive enough that the eye is stopped short of the problem being hidden.

Whatever features you introduce or have to cope with in your garden must be considered in the context of the garden as a whole. Features can add to a garden, yes, but their function is minor compared to the basic structure of a garden. On the other hand, the structures of some gardens are built up around one striking feature. Again, it all depends on who the gardener is and what he or she has to work with.

CHAPTER 9

Subtleties

Subtleties
help one
appreciate a
garden's
beauties after
the functional
decisions are
made.

After designing your garden, choosing plants to fit the growing conditions, maybe considering a theme for your garden and narrowing your choice of plants a little more, you might feel that that is a job well done and be quite content to finish there. If, on the other hand, you want to take into account more subtle design considerations, you could begin looking at shape, colour and texture before making your final choice of plants. It is far more important to have healthy plants of the right size and suited to their function, but the subtleties help one appreciate a garden's beauties after the functional decisions are made.

Shape

The shape of plants should have first consideration, because that is a plant's most obvious characteristic and is apparent all year round, particularly with evergreens. It also determines, to some extent, a plant's function. Vase shaped or upright trees and shrubs, such as Azaleas, Lilacs, Goldenrain Tree, Hackberry and some Crabapples, denote action and movement. Trees of this shape give a feeling of spaciousness, and people can also move under them freely. They are good as street trees, along driveways and near recreation areas. Many of the street trees listed in Table 1 are this shape. Upright shrubs function well as windbreaks, accents and narrow hedges, but they must be pruned carefully as hedges so that the bottom is not shaded out by the spreading top. They tend to be bare at the base and should be fronted by smaller rounded or spreading shrubs in a border.

Columnar and pyramidal plants, such as coniferous evergreens, command attention and are effective as accent plants. They tend to emphasize the vertical, so would be best avoided near tall, narrow houses. They could be used to emphasize a change of level, such as using a small pyramidal evergreen on either side of a short flight of steps, and they are also effective as screens in the form of a hedge, such as a row of Theve's Poplar.

Round and oval shapes, such as Norway Maple, Horse Chestnut, Rhododendrons and Shrub Roses, are good at blending horizontal and vertical masses, thereby creating unity and harmony in a garden. Round shrubs in front of leggy ones, for example, help to tie the upright plants to a flat expanse of groundcover or grass, and rounded trees and large shrubs help to tie a house to the ground. Round shrubs tend to take up a lot of space, but they look very good in an informal hedge and in shrub borders.

Irregular and spreading plants, such as Japanese Quince, Alternate-Leaf Dogwood, Corkscrew Hazel, some of the spreading Junipers and Cotoneasters, tend to be very picturesque and often have interesting winter outlines. They look good placed in front of tall plants, and they help to make tall structures, such as houses and walls, appear shorter and less imposing.

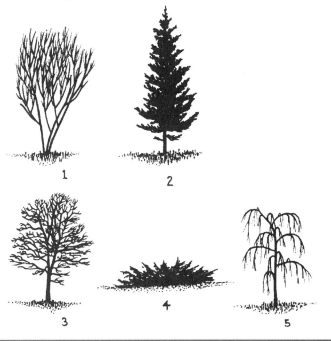

The shape of plants, in addition to height, determines their function. 1—Vase shaped or upright plants denote action and movement. 2—Columnar and pyramidal plants draw attention and act as accents. 3—Round and oval shapes make a good transition between vertical and horizontal masses. 4—Irregular and spreading plants are picturesque with their interesting outlines. 5—Arching and weeping forms create a restful atmosphere.

Arching and weeping forms, such as Garland Spirea, Weeping Forsythia, Weeping Nootka False Cypress, Pfitzer Juniper and Red Jade Crabapple, bring a relaxing, restful atmosphere to a garden. They draw the eye downward and work well beside or on top of walls, beside or behind seats, and at the edges of plant groups. They are also effective as accents or highlights because of their unusual form and the sudden change in shape from other plants.

It is best not to overuse specimens and accent plants, or they will detract from the focus of the garden and the unity of design. They will add interest, however, to what might otherwise be a flat, uninteresting design. Other than that, it is difficult to go far wrong in using plant shapes, especially as the suggested uses for plants in the earlier sections of the book take into account the various shapes for basic functions in a garden.

✑ Texture

Plant texture is determined mainly by the size of the leaves, and to some extent by the branches and twigs of a plant. Its main design use is matching plants to the scale of their surroundings, and in disguising distances. Contrasts in texture also add interest.

Coarse-leaved plants, such as Horse Chestnut, Catalpa, Oak, Rhododendrons, Dogwoods, Dutchman's Pipe and Hydrangeas, are better suited to large areas. If they are too close in a confined area, they seem overwhelming, but they can help to make a large area seem smaller. They are also effective at making a distance seem shorter, or bringing a far object nearer.

Fine-leaved plants, such as Birch, Honey-Locust, Willow, Hawthorn, Caragana, Cotoneaster, Ivy and Spirea, are more suited to small spaces and gardens. They tend to make near distances seem farther away.

When coarse and fine-leaved plants are used in conjunction with each other, useful illusions can result. Suppose, for example, that you have a short yard. Using coarser shrubs in the near distance and fine-leaved ones further away gives the illusion of greater depth. Perhaps you have a house with a prominent, protruding garage and a more distant, receding front door. The garage can be made to recede by using fine textured plants near it, and the front door brought forward and made prominent by the use of larger, coarse textured plants.

There is not always much choice when considering plant texture, especially if faced with difficult growing conditions, but there is sometimes room to play within a group of plants. Rhododendrons, for example, often have large, coarse leaves, but there are Rhododendrons with small, much finer leaves. The shrub rose Big John is a large plant with coarse leaves, but Kakwa is a smaller rose with finely divided leaves that has a much more delicate appearance.

Texture is something you might want to consider when narrowing your choice of plants for a particular function, especially when faced with deciding between several equally desirable plants. By the time you have considered plant shape as well, the plant to choose may be perfectly obvious.

Coarse leaved plants are suited to large areas and help to make distant plants seem closer. Fine leaved plants are suited to small or intimate areas and help to expand the sense of space. Used together, their contrast adds interest to the garden.

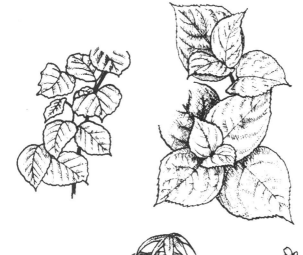

❧ Colour

Gardens and colour go hand in hand, yet for all its show, colour is not a substantial component of garden structure. It is very striking in season, however, and can have subtle effects on garden structure.

For private areas, cool colours, such as green, blue or purple, and soft shades of warm colours, such as peach, pink and quiet yellow, are more appropriate. For active areas, warm shades of red, orange and yellow are vibrant and more appropriate.

Colours can be used to alter perceptions of distance. Warm colours advance and cool colours recede. A short garden can be made to appear longer by placing warm colours close by and cool colours further away. A colour scheme of yellow, for example, would use bright yellow and strong orange nearby, and soft yellow and peach further away.

If mixing colours, larger masses of cool colours are needed to offset just a small patch of a warm colour. Lots of blue, for example, is needed to offset just a bit of red. The same quantity of blue, however, would offset larger amounts of soft yellows or pale pinks.

White is a good transition colour and, as mentioned previously, is particularly effective at night. White and green are effective as transitions between different colour groupings.

To get the most use out of colour, aim for a long sequence of change, using seasonal differences in all kinds of plants. Blooms of trees, shrubs, vines, perennials and bulbs are the most obvious sources of colour. Foliage of these plants, as well as that of ferns, grasses, and evergreens, provide tremendous variety in shades of green.

Some plants also have highly coloured foliage all through the summer and should be used sparingly, perhaps as accents. Plants with red or purple leaves include:

Bloodgood Japanese Maple	*Purple Smoketree*
Carmenetta Rose	*Royalty Crabapple*
Purple-leaf Sandcherry	*Shubert Chokecherry*
Purple-Leaved Weigela	*Spaeth Purple Beech*
Purple Japanese Maple	*Weeping Purple Beech*

Those with yellow foliage include:

Golden Elderberry	*Golden Mock Orange*
Golden Privet	*Goldmound Spirea*

Golden foliage is a clearer colour in sunny areas, but it is useful for brightening shady corners.

Other plants produce interesting shades in the spring as they first leaf out. A few examples are:

Amelanchier	*Goldflame Spirea*
Anthony Waterer Spirea	*Klondyke Azalea*
Champlain Rose	*Pieris*
Golden Ninebark	

Variegated plants have leaves edged or patterned with white, yellow, purple, pink, or lighter shades of green. They include Silverleaf and Yellowedge Dogwood, Pink Princess Weigela, Variegated Weigela, and *Euonymus fortunei* varieties. Use variegated plants with a light hand.

Twigs of many shrubs have strong, clear colours that are visible in winter, and these include: Carmenetta and Pink Surprise Rose, Siberian, Yellowedge, Silverleaf, and Red Osier Dogwood, (all have red stems), Yellowtwig Dogwood (yellow), Kerria (bright green), Common Sea Buckthorn (silvery), and Lace Shrub (a rich brown).

In planning your garden for all season interest, start planning for winter colour first, using evergreens and deciduous plants with coloured bark or interesting shapes, then look for autumn blooming plants or those with striking autumn foliage or berries. Many will probably have the bonus of spring blooms. Next, consider the plants with summer interest, those with flowers or unusual foliage. Finally, fit in some spring plants. Planning in this order will prevent an over abundance of spring blooming plants. For example, Forsythia is striking in spring, but quite uninteresting the rest of the year, whereas Blueberry has delicate spring flowers, blue berries in summer, striking red foliage in autumn, and yellow twigs in winter.

Using shape, texture and colour in your garden can work very well in adding to the sense of design. Light coloured plants and flowers in shady corners help to balance light and dark. Solid evergreens are heavier and more dominant than those with a lacey texture, so plant fewer heavy looking plants. Repetitions of a basic shape throughout the garden, with occasional changes for contrast, will tie the garden together. As well, placing plants in groups of three or five looks more balanced than groups of two or four, but this is not an unbendable rule. Plants with similar colouring or texture could be used at opposite ends or sides of a garden, giving balance as well as unity. It is mainly the use of repetition, with a few changes for interest and contrast, that give a garden a sense of wholeness.

There is such a lot to consider in assessing, planning, fine-tuning and planting a garden. Always, always, the basic function of plants and the appropriate growing conditions must have priority, but playing around with the subtle considerations is lots of fun.

CHAPTER 10

Action

Once you have completed your plan, the urge is to get on with the planting, but there is a logical order for accomplishing things in your design and costs might also be a consideration. If you plan to spread your activities over several years, you can rest assured that all the bits and pieces will fit into the total design, with the right action carried out at the right time.

There is a logical order for accomplishing things in your design

If you have a relatively bare lot or plan to do some major renovations in your yard, the rough grading and building of retaining walls and tree wells should be done first. Then you might consider doing the driveways and major paths in your design. Hire experts for this major work unless you are very confident and have lots of time or unless you have had previous experience. Ask around for reputable firms, and get several estimates before choosing a contractor if you decide to hire out this work.

Once this is done, topsoil can be brought in if necessary and the final shaping of land for drainage can be carried out. Construction of fences, patios, trellises and so on would be the next step. Lighting, too, would be considered at this time.

Once the heavy work is done, or if you are planning changes only to the planting in your garden, soil preparation can begin, as outlined in Chapter 6. This can be done in autumn so that everything is ready for a spring planting, especially important if buying bare root plants. It is discouraging to bring the plants home first and then have to rush to prepare the soil. You could also get the beds ready in the spring before you buy the plants so that you have a more realistic idea of how much you can accomplish in one season.

After you have listed all the plants you need and their costs, as well as the cost of soil amendments, mulches, and edgings, you might decide to do only part of the planting in any one year. That would also determine how much soil preparation is needed each year.

Trees are the biggest investment and take the longest to grow to an appreciable size, so they should be planted first. Groundcover is also needed to prevent erosion, so you might want to plant a cover crop or get your lawn established as soon as possible. There is no sense in hurrying the lawn, though, if you haven't determined the shape and position of planting areas around the yard. You could stake out the sites of future shrub borders, vegetable plots, and so on, and then plant your lawn around them, but the beds would need a cover crop or protection of some sort until they are planted. Instead of that, you could plant a cover crop over the entire area to tide you over until ready to plant the lawn. Cover crops such as winter wheat, oats, barley and annual rye could be planted in the fall and ploughed under in spring.

After the trees are in, shrubs are the next biggest planting. You might choose to do the foundation planting first, and then work your way to the less visible beds and those furthest from the house if you are spacing the planting over several years. You might decide, on the other hand, to plant the fruiting shrubs first and leave the more decorative ones until later, or plant deciduous plants first and the more expensive evergreens in later years. Temporary gaps can be filled in with flowers. Decide what is most important to you.

After the trees and shrubs come the groundcovers and lawn areas. Living groundcovers under trees and shrubs should not be planted for two or three years until the large plants are well established, but inanimate mulches can and should be spread immediately after planting.

Once the permanent plantings are in, attention can be given to the soft plantings, such as flower borders and vegetable plots. Again, if planting is spread over several years, you might want to make the vegetable plot a priority and save shrub plantings for a later date. As long as you know what your priorities are, and the cost considerations, you can plant in almost any order, provided the heavy disruptive work is taken care of first.

It is easy to take on more than can be readily managed, so it is very wise to do just a little bit of planting the first year to give you a more realistic notion of just how much work is involved in landscaping a yard. Getting the family involved helps a lot and is also very satisfying. You might decide to hire a landscaping firm, but you will have saved a lot of money just by doing the design yourself, and it will be far more individualized than what a commercial firm is likely to draw up for you.

Locating sources for the plants you want can be a real

Trees are the biggest investment and take the longest to grow to an appreciable size, so they should be planted first.

challenge. Nurseries know that many customers buy their plants in spring and are attracted to trees and shrubs in flower. Nurseries also want satisfied customers, so they stock plants that have a strong survival rate. This means that there is an excess of spring blooming, relatively common, easily grown, locally hardy plants, all of which are a boon for purple thumbers. This is one of the reasons for the preponderance of Junipers. Daphne, on the other hand, is sometimes difficult to come by because it requires a constantly moist soil and is not very long lived. In all fairness to nurseries, though, they cannot stock plants which do not sell; gardeners must ask for the plants they would like to try out.

The choice in plants, however, is expanding quite rapidly just now. Gardeners are becoming more discriminating and more knowledgeable, and there have been advances in recent years in plant propagation. Mountain Laurel, for example, used to be very difficult to propagate by traditional methods, but tissue culture has made it possible to reproduce large numbers. Hollies are also becoming more available. English and Chinese Hollies are too tender for Atlantic Canada; Japanese Holly is slightly hardier; Meservae hybrids, a cross between English and Japanese hollies, are moderately hardy, very attractive and very popular; Long Stalk and American Holly are hardier still; and the deciduous hollies, Mountain and Canada, are native and quite hardy. There are also specialty nurseries that have less well-known plants.

If your local nurseries do not have the plants you want, you could consider mail order. This can also save money because mail order firms send bare root stock, which is considerably less expensive than potted plants. It is very important, however, to buy from mail order sources that are located as near your area as possible. Plants from local sources are far more suited to the growing conditions, having been raised in those conditions themselves, and varieties have been selected for their suitability to the local climate. Smaller companies often give much better service and store their plants for shorter periods of time before mailing them out than do large companies. This ensures that gardeners receive fresh, good quality plants that stand a much better chance of surviving the rigours of the post office.

Whether you buy from local nurseries or mail order sources, try to find out if they propagate their own plants, or if not, from where they buy. It doesn't help much buying from a local nursery if the plants were imported from a warmer, milder climate than your own.

You might also consider propagating your own plants. If you can get cuttings or seeds from plants growing locally, or buy seeds of plants that are not readily available in local nurseries, you can save a lot of money and have a wider selection of plants. Larger seed companies often carry seeds of vines, shrubs, and trees. It might seem a lengthy process to grow a shrub from seed, but in three or four years you would have a plant comparable in size to nursery shrubs. Plant them outside as soon as they are of transplantable size after germinating, shelter them from drying winds, protect them very well the first one or two winters with generous mulching, and shrubs grown from seed will be very successful. Seed is also an inexpensive way of acquiring perennial flowers, although clumps can often be obtained from friendly neighbours and fellow gardeners.

Growing from cuttings is a particularly good way to provide yourself with a large number of plants for hedging or groundcovers. Sometimes you can purchase rooted cuttings from nursery catalogues. If you wanted a group of five Amur Maple, for example, you could purchase five potted plants for $85, five bare root plants for $65, or ten rooted cuttings (sold as hedge plants) for $25 at present prices. The potted and bare root plants would be larger, of course, but in a few years time there would be little difference in size, because large plants are slowed down in their growth when transplanted much more than small plants.

You could also dig up plants from the wild, as discussed in Chapter 2. Survival is often not good, if care has not been taken to root prune before moving plants, and permission from land owners must be sought.

Potted and bare root plants have been mentioned several times. Potted plants come with soil around their roots, and may be growing in plastic pots, in wooden baskets, or in pressed cellulose. Some plants are sold as ball and burlap, meaning that the root ball with soil is wrapped in burlap. When planting ball and burlap, or plants in wooden baskets, the covering need not be removed, although the burlap should be loosened from its twine. Both the burlap and wood are easily penetrated by roots, and both will rot readily. Plants

Growing from cuttings is a particularly good way to provide yourself with a large number of plants for hedging or groundcover.

must be removed from other containers before planting, however, and the root mass loosened with a garden claw or fork. If this is not done, the roots will sometimes remain in a tight ball and not grow out into the surrounding soil.

Bare root plants should be soaked in plain water for up to twelve hours before planting. If they cannot be planted immediately after their soaking, they should be placed in a trench in the garden and their roots covered with soil. This will hold them a short time until they can be planted in their permanent position.

Potted plants can be put in the ground at almost any time during the growing season. Bare root plants, on the other hand, can be planted only in early spring while they are still dormant, or in the autumn just after they lose their leaves. Reliable mail order sources will send bare root stock while it is still dormant, and good nurseries will also sell only dormant, bare root stock. Less reputable firms are not so careful. If you have a chance to see bare root stock before you buy it, make sure that no leafing out or flowering has taken place. If they have already leafed out, bare root plants are not likely to survive despite the best of care and attention in planting them.

In whatever form your plants arrive, make sure that you plant them at the same depth that they were growing in the nursery. The old soil line is usually visible, and a stick laid across the planting hole will ensure that the plants go in at the same level. A common cause of death of new trees and shrubs is planting too deeply. Soil amendments can be added to the planting hole, as discussed in Chapter 6, but if the soil is in generally good condition, this is not necessary. Make sure that the hole is twice as wide as the size of the root spread and the same depth as the container or root system. Deep rooted trees, such as Hackberry, American Linden (Basswood), Oaks, Ginkgo, Butternut and Tulip Tree, must have deep holes, up to 1 m deep.

Trim off broken, or damaged, or any overly long roots that are not tap roots. For container-grown plants, loosen the root mass and straighten out roots that are curling around the root ball. It is now considered undesirable to stake new trees with anything but a short, 30 cm stake, unless training a central leader for a fruit or weeping tree. A short stake keeps the plant upright but allows movement for the development of

strength. There is also no need to prune trees or shrubs except to remove damaged branches or to do a little shaping.

Regular deep watering on a weekly basis is essential for the survival of new plants. The best way is to run the hose at the rate of a trickle and leave it running for several hours or until the water puddles. A deep weekly watering like this is far more effective than a daily sprinkling, because it encourages the roots to grow out in their search for water instead of staying near the surface. The same holds for ground covers and newly sodded lawns, but freshly seeded lawns need daily moistening or to be kept moist with a covering of burlap or weed free straw until the seed has germinated. Deep weekly waterings start once the new lawn has grown 3 cm.

Regular watering and shelter from winter winds is particularly important for plants set out in autumn. It is also a help to mulch the ground before freeze up so that roots have more time to get established. Two advantages to autumn planting is that plants are often sold at reduced prices, and nursery personnel have more time to give individual attention to customers. It is best not to plant in the autumn in very windy situations, however, unless great care is taken in building shelters for the new plants. Even in sites that aren't windy, tender plants should also be sheltered for the first two or three years until well established.

There is a lot to be done, but gardens and gardening need to be savoured.

Putting in the plants is a pleasure after all the care in planning the design and choosing the right plants. Preparing the soil well in advance and spreading out the planting over several months or several years will extend this rewarding activity. Plants take time to grow, and gardeners do well when they attune their efforts and expectations to the pace of the plants.

Just as a gardener's dreams and visions are ever developing, so is the garden. The site may be altered, the gardener's needs and abilities will change, new plants will be developed. Gardens are living entities and, like people, they mellow and mature and develop more character with each passing season.

Zone Map

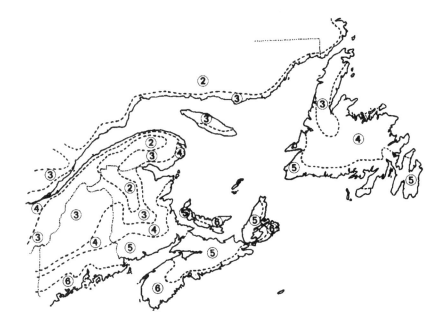

TABLE 1 • 151

Tables

Table 1

Trees Suitable for Lawn, Patio, Specimen and Street Planting

Light * requires at least 8 hours of sunlight daily
           + requires 4 hours or more of sunlight daily; also tolerates dappled shade;
           - tolerates less than 4 hours of sunlight daily
Shade cast   d: dense; m: medium; l: light
!   good all season plants
upright varieties best

zone	light		shade	lawn	patio	specimen	street	interest
Up to 6 m								
2	* +	Amur Maple	m		x		x	!
2	*	Russian Olive	m			x		!
2	* + -	Wayfaring Tree (*V.lantana*)	d			x		
2	* +	Young's Weeping Birch	m		x	x		
3	+ -	American Hornbeam (Blue Beech)	m		x			
3,4	*	Flowering Crabapples	l			x	#x	!
3	* +	Chinese Paper Birch	m		x			!
3	* +	Gray (Wire) Birch	m		x			
3	* + -	Hop Hornbeam (Ironwood)	m				x	
3	* +	Japanese Tree Lilac	m		x	x	x	
3	*	Peegee Hydrangea	m			x		!
3	*	Purple-Leaf Sandcherry	l		x	x		!
3	*	Sumac: Staghorn, Dissecta, Chinese	l			x		!
3	* +	Weeping Mulberry	m		x	x		!
4	+ -	Alternate-Leaf Dogwood	m		x	x		!
3,4	* +	Amelanchier	m		x		x	!
4	*	Hawthorns	l	x		x	x	!
5	* +	Angelica (Devil's Walking Stick)	l			x		
5	*	Bradford Callery Pear	m	x	x	x	x	!
5	* +	Chinese Flowering Dogwood	l			x		!
5	* +	Cornelian Cherry (*Cornus mas*)	l			x		!
5	* +	Eastern Redbud (*Cercis,* Judas Tree)	m		x			!
5	*	Fringetree (*Chionanthus*)	l	x	x	x		!
5	* +	Magnolia: Saucer, Oyama	l		x	x		!

zone	light		shade	lawn	patio	specimen	street	interest
5	*	Umbrella Catalpa	m			x		
6	* +	Golden Chain Tree (Laburnum)	l	x	x	x		
6	*	Goldenrain Tree (Koelreuteria)	l			x		
6	+ -	Japanese Maple	m	x	x	x		!
6	*	Kwanzan (Japanese) Cherry	m			x		
6	*	Weeping Japanese Cherry	m		x	x		
Up to 15 m								
2	* +	Cutleaf Weeping Birch	m			x		
2	* +	Himalayan Birch	m			x		!
3	*	Amur Cork	l	x	x			!
3	*	European Mountain Ash (Rowan)	m	x	x	x	x	!
3	*	Little-Leaf Linden & varieties	d	x		x		
3	* +	Ohio Buckeye	m			x	x	
3	* +	Red Maple	m			x		
3	*	Siberian Pear	m	x	x	x	x	!
4	*	Black Locust	m			x		!
4	*	Honey-Locust	l	x	x	x		
4	* +	Ruby Horse Chestnut	d			x	x	
5	* +	Globe Norway Maple	d			x		
5	*	Kentucky Coffee Tree	m	x		x		!
6	*	Beech: Copper, Spaeth Purple	m			x		!
6	*	Chinese Chestnut	m			x		
6	*	Zelkova	m	x		x		
15 m or More								
2	* +	American Linden (Basswood)	m			x	x	
2	* +	Birch: Paper, Silver	l			x		!
2	*	Green Ash	l	x		x		
2	* +	River (Silver, White) Maple	m			x		
3	*	Hackberry	m	x				!
3	*	White Ash	l			x		
3	*	White Willow	m			x		
3,4	*	Oak: English, Pin, Red	m	x		x	x	
4	*	American Beech	m			x		
4	* +	Black (Red, River) Birch	l			x		
4	* +	Common Horse Chestnut	d			x		

TABLE 1 • 153

zone	light		shade	lawn	patio	specimen	street	interest
4	* +	Ginkgo	m	x		x		!
4	* +	Sugar Maple	d			x		
5	* +	Northern Catalpa	m	x				
5	* +	Norway Maple	d				x	
5	*	Tulip	d	x				!

TABLE 2

Plants Suitable for Hedges, Windbreaks, Screens and Shrub Borders

Light * requires at least 8 hours of sunlight daily;
+ requires 4 or more hours of sunlight daily; also tolerates dappled shade;
- tolerates less than 4 hours of sunlight daily
Growth rate f: fast; m: medium; s: slow—plants grow taller in mild zones
!   good all season plants

zone	light		growth rate	hedge (formal/ informal)	wind break	screen	shrub border	interest
Deciduous, up to 0.6 m								
3,4	*	Shrub Roses	f	i			x	!
4	* +	Cotoneaster: Creeping, Praecox	f				x	!
4	* +	Spirea: Little Princess, Bullata	m	i			x	!
5	*	Helianthemum (Rock Rose)	m				x	!
5	*	Lavender	m	f i				
5	*	Purple Broom	m				x	
5	*	Sage	m				x	!
5	*	*Stephanandra incisa* 'Crispa'	m				x	
6	*	Rosemary	m	f i				
6	* +	St. John's Wort	m	i				!
Broad-Leaved Evergreens, up to 0.6 m								
1	* +	Lambkill (Sheep's Laurel)	m				x	
2	* +	Bog Rosemary	m				x	
3	*	Garland Flower *(Daphne cneorum)*	s				x	!
3	*	Iberis (Evergreen Candytuft)	s				x	
3	+ -	Japanese Spurge	m				x	
4	* +	Cliff Green *(Pachystima)*	m	i			x	
4,5	*	Heaths, Heathers	s				x	!
4	* +	Small Leaved Rhododendrons	s				x	
5	* + -	Pincushion Box	s				x	
6	* + -	Green Gem Box	s	f i			x	
Coniferous Evergreens, up to 0.6 m								
3	* +	Globe Cedar: Danica, Little Giant	s	f i			x	
4	*	Dwarf Balsam Fir	s				x	
4	*	Dwarf Alberta Globe Spruce	s				x	
6	* +	Dwarf Hinoki False Cypress	s				x	

TABLE 2 • 155

zone	light		growth rate	hedge (formal/informal)	wind break	screen	shrub border	interest
Deciduous, up to 1.2 m								
2	* +	Anthony Waterer Spirea	f	i			x	!
2	* +	Arctic (Basket) Willow	f	f i			x	
2	* +	Cinquefoil (Potentilla)	f	f i	x		x	
2	*	Clavey's Dwarf Honeysuckle	m	f i	x		x	
2	*	Dart's Ninebark	m	f i			x	
2	*	Dwarf Korean Lilac	m	i			x	
2	*	Pygmy Caragana	m	f i			x	
3	* + -	Annabelle Hydrangea	f	i			x	!
3	* +	Dwarf Burning Bush	m	f i			x	!
3	* +	February Daphne (*D.mezereum*)	s				x	!
3,4	*	Shrub Roses	f	i			x	!
3	* +	Spirea: Goldflame, Goldmound	f	i			x	!
3	* +	Troost Birch	m				x	!
4	*	Double Flowering Almond	f				x	
4	*	Floribunda Roses	f	i				
4	* +	Red Chokeberry	f	f i			x	!
4	* +	Snowbelle Mock Orange	m				x	
5	* +	Burkwood Daphne	s				x	!
5	*	Japanese Quince (*C.japonica*)	m	f i			x	!
6	*	Allgold Broom	m	i	x		x	!
6	* +	Bigleaf, Lacecap Hydrangea	f				x	!
6	* +	Oakleaf Hydrangea	f				x	!
Broad-Leaved Evergreens, up to 1.2 m								
3	* +	Leatherleaf (*Chamaedaphne*)	m				x	
4	* +	PJM Rhododendron	s				x	
5	+ -	Mahonia	s	f i			x	!
5	* + -	Winter Beauty Korean Box	s	f i			x	
5,6	* + -	Euonymus fortunei	m				x	
6	* +	Azalea: Kurume, Kaempferi	s				x	!
6	+	Drooping Leucothoe	s				x	!
5,6	* +	Holly	s	f i			x	!
Coniferous Evergreens, up to 1.2 m								
1	*	Dwarf Mugo Pine	s				x	
2	*	Compact Andorra Juniper	s				x	

zone	light		growth rate	hedge (formal/ informal)	wind break	screen	shrub border	interest
3	* +	Globe Cedar: Little Champion	s	f i			x	
3	*	Dwarf Blue Spruce	s				x	
4	* +	Jeddeloh Hemlock	s				x	
4,5	*	Junipers: spreading vars.	m				x	
5	* + -	Dense Yew	s	f i			x	i

Deciduous, up to 2 m

zone	light		growth rate	hedge (formal/ informal)	wind break	screen	shrub border	interest
2	* +	Dogwoods	m				x	!
2	*	Dwarf Korean Lilac	m	i	x		x	
2	* + -	False Spirea	f				x	
2	*	Golden Ninebark	f	f i	x	x	x	
2	* +	Peking (pointed) Cotoneaster	f		x	x		
2	* + -	Snowberry (Waxberry)	m	i			x	
2	*	Weeping Caragana	f			x		
3	* + -	Alpine (Flowering) Currant	m	f i				
3	* +	Bayberry	m	f i	x		x	
3	* +	Canada Holly (Winterberry)	m				x	!
3	+	Mountain (Wild) Holly	m				x	
3,4	*	Dwarf Flowering Crabapples	m	i		x	x	!
3,4	* +	Mock Orange: Purity, Snowflake, Buckley's Quill	f	f i			x	
3,4	* +	Spirea: Garland, Bridal Wreath	f	i			x	
3,4	*	Shrub Roses	f	i			x	!
4	* +	Cotoneaster salicifolius	m	f i			x	!
4	* +	Forsythia: Ottawa, N. Gold	f	i	x		x	
4	* +	Highbush Blueberry	m	i			x	!
4	* +	Morrow Honeysuckle	f	i		x		
4	*	Persian Lilac	f	i		x	x	
4,5	*	Weigelas	m				x	
5	* +	Azaleas	m				x	
5	*	Butterfly Bush	f				x	
5	*	Common (Flowering) Quince	m	f i			x	
5	* +	Compact Lemoine Deutzia	m			x	x	
5	+	Enkianthus	m				x	!

TABLE 2 • 157

zone	light		growth rate	hedge (formal/ informal)	wind break	screen	shrub border	interest
5	* + -	Five-Leaved Aralia	f	f i	x			
5	*	Golden Privet	f	f i	x			!
5	* + -	Kerria	m				x	
5	* +	Lace Shrub (Stephanandra)	m				x	
5	* +	Viburnum: K. Spice, Burkwood	s				x	!
6	+ -	Cutleaf Purple Japanese Maple	s				x	!
6	* +	Hibiscus (Rose of Sharon)	s				x	!

Broad-Leaved Evergreens, up to 2 m

zone	light		growth rate	hedge	wind break	screen	shrub border	interest
5	* + -	Mountain Laurel (Kalmia)	s				x	!
5	+	Mountain Pieris (Pieris floribunda)	s	i			x	!
5,6	* +	Rhododendrons	s				x	
5	* + -	Sarcoxie Euonymus	m	f i			x	
5	* + -	Tall Boy Box	s	f i			x	
6	* +	Firethorn (Pyracantha)	m	f i		x	x	!
5,6	* +	Holly	s	f i		x	x	!
6	+	Lily-of-the-Valley Shrub(P. japonica)	s	f i			x	!

Coniferous Evergreens, up to 2 m

zone	light		growth rate	hedge	wind break	screen	shrub border	interest
1	*	Pumilio Mugo Pine	s				x	
2	*	Bird's Nest Spruce	s				x	
3	*	Dwarf Rocky Mountain Fir	s				x	
3	*	Ohlendorff Spruce	m				x	
4	*	Dwarf Alberta Spruce	s				x	
4	* +	Fernspray Cypress	m				x	
4	*	Juniper: vase-shaped vars.	m	f i			x	
4	* + -	Yew: Dwarf Japanese, Dark Green	s	f			x	!
5	* +	Dwarf Hinoki False Cypress	s	i			x	
5	* +	Sawara F. Cypress aurea nana	s	i			x	

Deciduous, up to 3 m

zone	light		growth rate	hedge	wind break	screen	shrub border	interest
2	*	Nanking Cherry	m	f i			x	
2	* +	Ninebark	f		x	x		
2	* +	Peking (Pointed) Cotoneaster	f	f i	x	x		
2	*	Preston Lilac	f	i	x	x		
2	*	Russian Olive	m	f i	x			

zone	light		growth rate	hedge (formal/ informal)	wind break	screen	shrub border	interest
2	* +	Tatarian Honeysuckle	f	f i	x	x	x	
3	*	Common Lilac, Chinese Lilac	f	i	x	x		
3	* +	Burning Bush	f	f i		x	x	!
3	* +	Common Sea Buckthorn	f	f i	x			
3	* + -	Elderberry	f	i	x	x	x	!
3	* +	Flowering Almond	m				x	
3	* +	Sweet Mock Orange	f	f i	x		x	
3	*	Tamarix: Feathery, 5-Stamen	m	i				
4	*	Myer Lilac, Persian Lilac	f	i	x	x		
4	*	Privets	f	f i	x			
4	* +	Virginal Mock Orange	f		x		x	
4,5	* +	Spirea: Snowmound, Pink	f	i			x	
5	*	Beauty Bush (Kolkwitzia)	s				x	
5	* +	Corkscrew Hazel	m				x	!
5	* +	Forsythia: upright	f	i	x		x	
5	* +	Forsythia: weeping	f	i			x	
5	*	Magnolia: Star, Oyama	s				x	!
5	*	Smoke Tree	s				x	!
6	* +	Eastern Redbud (Cercis)	m				x	!
6	* +	Fragrant Snowball Viburnum	s				x	!
6	+ -	Japanese Maple	s				x	!

Broad-Leaved Evergreens, up to 3 m

zone	light		growth rate	hedge	wind break	screen	shrub border	interest
5,6	* +	Rhododendrons	s				x	

Coniferous Evergreens, up to 3 m

zone	light		growth rate	hedge	wind break	screen	shrub border	interest
2	*	Bristlecone Pine	s		x	x		
3	* +	Cedar (Thuja): upright vars.	m	f i		x	x	
4	* +	Hemlock: Calvert, Pomfret	s	f i		x	x	
4,5	*	Junipers: upright varieties	m	f i	x	x	x	
4	*	Korean Fir	s	i		x	x	
4,5	* + -	Yew: Hick's, Hill's	s	f i		x	x	!
5	* +	Blue Cone Cedar	m				x	
5	* +	False Cypress: upright vars.	m	i			x	

Deciduous, up to 6 m

zone	light		growth rate	hedge	wind break	screen	shrub border	interest
2	* +	Amur Maple	m	f i	x	x		!
2	*	Bird (Pin) Cherry	f		x		x	!

TABLE 2 • 159

zone	light		growth rate	hedge (formal/ informal)	wind break	screen	shrub border	interest
2	*	Caragana	m	f i	x	x		
2	*	Choke Cherry	f		x	x		
2	* +	Common Witch Hazel	m				x	!
2	* +	(European) Snowball Viburnum	m	f i		x	x	
2	* +	Highbush Cranberry (V.trilobum)	m			x	x	!
2	* +	Nannyberry (V.lentago)	m	f i		x	x	!
2	*	Russian Olive	m	f i	x			
2	* + -	Wayfaring Tree (V.lantana)	m	i			x	!
3,4	* +	Amelanchier	m	f i	x	x		!
3	+ -	American Hornbeam (Blue Beech)	m	f i		x		
3	* +	Black Mulberry	m			x		
3	* +	Gray (Wire) Birch	f			x		
3	* +	Japanese Tree Lilac	f		x			
3	*	Purple-Leaf Sandcherry	m	i		x	x	
3,4	*	Crabapples	m			x		!
4	+ -	Alternate-Leaf Dogwood	m				x	!
4	*	Hawthorns	m	f i			x	!
5	*	Bradford Callery Pear	m		x		x	
5	* +	Chinese Flowering Dogwood	m				x	!
5	* +	Cornelian Cherry (Cornus mas)	m		x	x	x	!
6	*	Beech: Copper, Spaeth Purple	s	f i		x	x	!
6	* +	Pyramidal European Hornbeam	m	f i	x			

Coniferous Evergreens, up to 6 m

zone	light		growth rate	hedge (formal/ informal)	wind break	screen	shrub border	interest
2	*	Swiss Stone Pine	m	f i	x	x		
3	*	Eastern Red Cedar (Juniper)	m	f i	x	x		
3	*	Serbian Spruce	m	f i	x	x		
3	* +	Thuja: upright Cedars	m	f i		x	x	
4	*	Juniper: upright varieties	m	f i	x	x	x	
4	*	Korean Fir	s			x		
4,5	* +	False Cypress: G.Hinoki, Threadleaf	s	i				
4,5	* + -	Yew: Hick's, Hill's, Upr. Jap.	s	f i		x	x	!

Deciduous, up to 15 m or more

zone	light		growth rate	hedge (formal/ informal)	wind break	screen	shrub border	interest
2	* +	Cutleaf Weeping Birch	f			x		!
2	*	Berlin Poplar and others	f		x			
2	*	Green Ash	f		x			

zone	light		growth rate	hedge (formal/informal)	wind break	screen	shrub border	interest
2	*	Silver (White) Poplar	f			x		
2	* +	Sycamore Maple	m		x			
3	*	Bolleana Poplar	f			x		
3	*	Little-Leaf Linden	m		x			
3	*	Siberian Pear	m		x			!
3	*	White Willow	f		x			
3,4	* +	Maples	f		x			!
6	*	Zelkova	m		x			
Coniferous Evergreens, up to 15 m								
3	* +	American Larch (L.laricina)	m	f i				
3	*	Serbian Spruce	m	f i	x	x		
3	* +	Thuja (White Cedar)	m	f i		x		
4	*	Austrian Pine	f			x		
4	* +	Sawara False Cypress	s	f i				
5	*	Korean Pine	f			x		
6	* +	Leyland Cypress	s	f i		x		
Coniferous Evergreens, 15 m or more								
1	*	White Spruce	s	f i	x	x		
2	*	Balsam Fir	m	f i		x		
2	*	Colorado Blue Spruce	m	f i	x	x		
2	*	Common (Norway) Spruce	f	f i		x		
2	*	White Pine	f	f i				
3	*	Eastern Red Cedar	m	f i	x	x		
3	* +	European Larch (L.decidua)	m	f i				
4	* +	Canadian (Eastern) Hemlock	f	f i		x		
4	*	Douglas Fir	m	f i				

N.B. Larches are deciduous, but they are coniferous in shape and function

TABLE 3 • 161

Table 3

Plants to Grow with Walls

Height: in metres
On top: may be grown on top of walls
Espalier: may be espaliered
Light * requires at least 8 hours of sunlight daily;
         + requires 4 or more hours of sunlight daily; also tolerates dappled shade;
         - tolerates less than 4 hours of sunlight daily
!   good all season plants

zone	light		height	espalier	on top	interest
Deciduous						
2	*	Dyer's Greenwood *(Genista tinctoria)*	0.3		x	
3	*	Cane Fruits: Raspberries, Brambles	2.0	x		
3	* +	Flowering Almond	5.0	x		
3,4	*	Apple	5.0	x		
3,4	*	Shrub Roses: spreading varieties	0.6		x	!
		Shrub Roses to tie up	3.0	x		!
3	*	Siberian Pear	5.0	x		!
3	*	Tamarix: Feathery, 5-Stamen	5.0	x		
4	*	*Genista pilosa, G. sagittalis* (Broom)	0.3		x	
4	* + -	Kerria	2.0	x		!
4	*	Pear	5.0	x		
4	* +	*Cotoneaster adpressus:* Praecox, Creeping	0.3		x	!
5	* +	*Cotoneaster horizontalis* (rockspray)	0.6	x	x	!
5	* +	*Cotoneaster salicifolius*	2.0	x		!
5	*	Bradford Callery Pear	5.0	x		
5	*	Flowering Quince *(C. speciosa)*	2.0	x		!
5	*	Helianthemum (Rock Rose)	0.3		x	
5	*	Japanese Quince *(C. japonica)*	1.2	x		!
5	* +	Saucer Magnolia	5.0	x		
5	* +	Weeping Forsythia	3.0	x		
6	*	Allgold Broom and other varieties	1.2	x	x	!
6	*	Climbing Roses	3.0	x		
6	* +	Golden Chain Tree *(Laburnum)*	5.0	x		
6	* +	Rose of Sharon *(Hibiscus syriacus)*	2.0	x		!

zone	light		height	espalier	on top	interest
6	*	Peach	5.0	x		
6	* +	St. John's Wort	0.3		x	!
Evergreen						
1	* +	Bearberry *(Arctostaphylos)*	0.3		x	!
2	* +	Microbiota	0.3		x	
3	*	Garland Flower *(Daphne cneorum)*	0.3		x	!
3	*	Iberis (Evergreen Candytuft)	0.3		x	
3	*	Juniper: low or creeping varieties	0.3		x	
3	* + -	Vinca minor (Periwinkle)	0.3		x	!
4	* +	*Cotoneaster dammeri* (Bearberry)	0.3	x	x	!
5	* +	*Cotoneaster dammeri* 'Coral Beauty'	0.3	x	x	!
5	* +	*Cotoneaster microphyllus* (Littleleaf)	0.6	x	x	!
5	* + -	Sarcoxie Euonymus	2.0	x		
5	* + -	Wintercreeper	1.0	x	x	
5	* + -	Yews	2.0	x		!
6	* + -	English Ivy 'Baltica'	1.0	x	x	!
6	* +	Holly	2.0	x		!
6	* +	Pyracantha (Firethorn)	2.0	x		!

TABLE 4 • 163

Table 4

Vines for Every Situation

Light * requires at least 8 hours of sunlight daily;
       + requires 4 or more hours of sunlight daily; also tolerates dappled shade;
       - tolerates less than 4 hours of sunlight daily
! good all season plants
Growth rate: s: slow; reaches ultimate height of 1m to 4m;
                m: moderate; reaches up to 8m
                f: fast; reaches 15m or more
Attachment: c: climbs by clinging;   t: climbs by twining ;   o: must be tied
Trees: vines may be grown climbing into trees or tall shrubs
tp: tender perennial
a: annual

zone	light		growth rate	attach	flowers	trees	interest
Deciduous							
3,4	* +	Bittersweet	m	t			
3,5	*	Grape	f	t		x	!
3,5	* +	Honeysuckles	m	t	various		!
3	* + -	Virginia Creeper	f	ct			
4	*	Actinidia (Hardy Kiwi)	m	t			!
4,5	* +	Clematis: Hybrids, Species	s	t	various	x	!
4	* +	Silver Lace Vine	f	t	white		!
4	*	Shrub Roses	s	o	various		!
5	* + -	Boston Ivy	f	c			
5	* + -	Climbing Hydrangea	s	c	white	x	!
5	* +	Dutchman's Pipe	m	t	brown	x	
5	* + -	Five-Leaf Akebia	m	t	purple		!
5	*	Trumpet Vine *(Campsis)*	f	ct	orange		!
5	*	Wisteria	f	t	purple	x	!
6	*	Climbing Roses	s	o	various		!
Evergreen							
5	* + -	Wintercreeper	s	c			
5	* + -	Sarcoxie Euonymus	s	o			
6	* + -	English Ivy 'Baltic'	s	c			!

Annual/Tender Perennial

zone	light		growth rate	attach	flowers	trees	interest
tp	+	Balloon	s	c	green	x	
tp	+	Brown-Eyed Susan	s	t	yellow		
a	*	Bottle Gourd	f	c	white	x	
a	*	Canary Creeper	s	o	yellow		
tp	* +	Chilean Glory Flower	s	c	various	x	
tp	*	Creeping Gloxinia	s	t	various	x	
tp	*	Cup and Saucer	f	c	purple	x	
a	*	Cypress	f	t	red, white		
tp	*	Hyacinth Bean	m	t	purple, white		
tp	*	Japanese Hop	m	t			
a	+	Moonflower	m	t	white		
a	* +	Morning Glory	s	t	various		
a	* +	Nasturtium	s	o	various		
a	+	Purple Bell	s	t	purple		
a	*	Sweet Pea	s	t	various		

Based on information in *Annual Garden* by Jennifer Bennett and Turid Forsyth, Camden House, 1990.

TABLE 5 • 165

Table 5
Recommended Pruning Times

Prune While Dormant

Actinidia (Hardy Kiwi)
Amelanchier
Butterfly Bush
Clematis
Dogwood - for coloured bark
Elderberry
English Ivy
Euonymus
Five-Leaved Aralia
Flowering Raspberry
Grape
Heather - fall blooming
Honeysuckle: shrub, climbing
Hydrangea: climbing, *arborescens*, Annabelle,
    Hills-of-Snow, Peegee, Grandiflora
Japanese Tree Lilac
Privet
Rose of Sharon *(Hibiscus syriacus)*
Roses - recurrent, shrub
Silver Lace Vine
Snowberry (Waxball)
Sorbaria (False Spirea)
Spirea: Anthony Waterer, Bullata,
    Little Princess, Snowmound, Pink,
    Goldflame, Goldmound
St. John's Wort
Sumac
Tamarix: 5-Stamen
Trumpet Creeper *(Campsis)*
Viburnum - for berries
Willow
Witch Hazel, Common

Prune After Blooming

Azalea
Beautybush *(Kolkwitzia)*
Bittersweet *(Celastris)*
Broom
Caragana (Siberian Pea Shrub)
Cinquefoil (Potentilla)
Cytisus
Daphne
Deutzia
Eastern Redbud *(Cercis)*
English Hawthorn
Five-Leaf Akebia
Flowering Currant
Flowering Dogwood
Flowering, Japanese Quince
Forsythia
Fringe Tree
Genista
Heath - spring blooming
Helianthemum (Rock Rose)
Hydrangea: Macrophylla, Bigleaf,
    Lacecap, Mophead, Oakleaf
Kerria
Lavender
Lilac
Magnolia
Mock Orange *(Philadelphus)*
Mountain Laurel (Kalmia)
Ninebark
Pieris
Prunus: Flowering Almond,
    Flowering Cherry, Flowering
    Plum
Rhododendron
Roses: climbing, rambler,
    single-blooming
Smoke Tree
Spirea: Bridal Wreath, *vanhouttei,*
    Garland, *arguta,* Snowmound
Stephanandra
Tamarix: Feathery
Viburnum: Fragrant, Korean Spice,
    Burkwood, Wayfaring Tree
Virginia Creeper
Weigela
Wisteria

Table 6

Plants Suitable as Groundcovers

Light	* requires at least 8 hours of sunlight daily;
	+ requires 4 or more hours of sunlight daily, tolerates dappled shade;
	- tolerates less than 4 hours of sunlight daily
dry:	needs dry conditions
slope:	will grow on slope
foot traffic:	tolerates foot traffic: x: yes; o: occasionally
!	good all season plants

zone	light		dry	slope	lawn substitute	foot traffic	interest
Perennials							
2	* +	Pinks (Dianthus deltoides)		x	x		!
2	*	Moss Pink (Phlox subulata)	x	x		o	!
2	*	Thrift (Armeria)	x			o	
3	*	Arabis (Rock Cress)	x			o	!
3	* +	Chamomile	x		x	x	
3	* +	Daylilies		x			!
3	* + -	Ferns					!
3	* + -	Fringed Bleeding Heart					
3	* +	Geranium (Cranesbill)					
3	*	Lamb's Ear (Stachys)	x				
3	+	Lily-of-the-Valley					
3	*	Snow-in-Summer (Cerastium)	x	x		o	
4	* + -	Ajuga (Bugleweed)				x	
4	* +	Bergenia	x				!
4	+ -	Hosta		x			
4	*	Potentilla			x	o	
4	*	Sedum (Stonecrop)	x	x	x		
4	* +	Sweetfern (Comptonia)	x				
4	* +	Violets					
4	+ -	Wild Ginger (Asarum)					
4	*	Wooly Thyme	x		x	x	
5	+ -	Forget-me-Not				•	
3,5	*	Ornamental Grasses	x	x	x		

TABLE 6 • 167

zone	light		dry	slope	lawn substitute	foot traffic	interest
Deciduous, up to 0.6 m							
2	*	Dyer's Greenwood (Broom)		x			
3	*	Shrub Roses		x			!
4	* +	*Cotoneaster adpressus*		x			!
4	*	Genista (Broom)	x	x			
4	* +	Spirea: Little Princess, Bullata		x			!
5	* +	*Cotoneaster horizontalis* (Rockspray)		x			!
5	*	Helianthemum (Rock Rose)	x	x			!
5	*	Lavender	x				!
5	*	Purple Broom	x	x			
5	*	Sage	x				!
5	*	*Stephanandra incisa* 'Crispa'					
6	* +	Rosemary	x				
6	* +	St. John's Wort	x	x	x		!
6	*	Spanish Gorse	x	x			
Evergreen, up to 0.6 m							
1	* +	Bearberry *(Arctostaphylos)*	x	x			!
2	* +	Lambkill					
2	* +	Microbiota		x			
3	* + -	Canada Yew (Ground Hemlock)		x			
3	* +	Huckleberry		x			!
3	*	Iberis (Evergreen Candytuft)					
3	+ -	Japanese Spurge			x		
3	* + -	*Vinca minor* (Periwinkle)	x	x		o	!
4	* +	Cliff Green *(Pachystima)*	x	x			
4	* +	*Cotoneaster dammeri* (Bearberry)	x	x			!
4	* +	Creeping Thyme	x			o	
4	*	Heath, Heathers		x			!
4	*	Juniper: creeping varieties	x	x	x	x	
5	* +	*Cotoneaster dammeri* 'Coral Beauty'	x	x			!
5	* +	*Cotoneaster microphyllus* (Little-Leaf)	x	x			
5	+	Leucothoe					!
Vines							
3,4	* +	Bittersweet					!
3	*	Crown Vetch	x	x	x		

zone	light		dry	slope	lawn substitute	foot traffic	interest
3,4	*	Grape					!
3	* + -	Virginia Creeper	x	x			
4	*	Golden Clematis (C. tangutica)		x		!	
4	*	Silver Lace Vine	x	x			!
4,5	* +	Honeysuckle		x	x		!
5	* + -	Boston Ivy	x	x			
5	* + -	Climbing Hydrangea	x	x			!
5	* +	Five-Leaf Akebia		x			!
5	* + -	Wintercreeper		x			
6	* + -	English Ivy 'Baltica'		x	x		!
6	* +	Sweet Autumn Clematis		x			!

Deciduous, up to 1.2 m

zone	light		dry	slope	lawn substitute	foot traffic	interest
2	* +	Anthony Waterer Spirea	x	x			!
2	*	Cinquefoil (Potentilla)	x				
3	*	Shrub Roses					!
3	* +	Spirea: Goldflame, Goldmound	x	x			!
5	*	Japanese Quince (C. japonica)	x	x			!
6	*	Allgold Broom	x	x			!

Evergreen, up to 1.2 m

zone	light		dry	slope	lawn substitute	foot traffic	interest
4	*	Juniper: spreading varieties	x				
5	+ -	Mahonia					!

Deciduous, up to 2 m

zone	light		dry	slope	lawn substitute	foot traffic	interest
2	* + -	False Spirea		x			!
2	* +	Red Osier Dogwood		x			!
2	* +	Dogwood: others					!
3	*	Shrub Roses					!
4	* +	Morrow Honeysuckle		x			
5	* +	Deutzia		x			
5	*	Flowering Quince (C. speciosa)	x	x			!
5	* +	Stephanandra (Lace Shrub)		x			
5	* +	Weeping Forsythia		x			

Evergreen, up to 2 m

zone	light		dry	slope	lawn substitute	foot traffic	interest
4	*	Juniper: spreading varieties	x				
4	* + -	Yew: spreading varieties					!
5	* + -	Mountain Laurel (Kalmia)		x			!

TABLE 7 • 169

Table 7
Lawn Grasses

Grass	Characteristics	Growing Conditions
Kentucky Bluegrass	- slow to germinate - easy care - mows beautifully - hard wearing - spreads by creeping - no poor soil	- no extremes of pH - good for light soil - drought resistant - disease resistant - no shade or wetness
Perennial Ryegrass	- germinates quickly - hides coarse grass - tolerates neglect - mows moderately well - does not spread	- tolerates heavy soil - no extremes of climate - grows quickly,needs frequent mowing
Annual Ryegrass	- starts quickly, dies out mostly in one year. - mixed with other grasses to provide quick cover until slower grasses become established, or used as cover crop.	

Coarse Fescue	- very rugged
	- does not blend well
	  with other grasses
		- tolerates wide range of growing
		  conditions
		- resistant to drought
		- resistant to disease

Fine Fescues	- chewing fescues are
	  very dense
	- creeping fescues
	  stabilize soil
	- looks luxurious
	- germinates quickly
	- is expensive
		- tolerate dry conditions
		- tolerate poor soil
		- will grow in shade

Bent Grass	- does not tolerate
	  neglect
	- slow to establish
	- does not hide coarse
	  grasses
	- can't take hard wear
	- is expensive
	- looks luxurious
		- susceptible to disease
		- requires frequent mowing
		- spreads by creeping
		- likes humid climates
		- requires careful preparation of soil
		- tolerates light shade

Clover	- a legume - does not look smooth - little maintenance	- requires no fertilizer - stays green in drought - mix 20% to 50% with grass seed

Most lawn grasses are sold as mixtures for various functions: luxury lawns, play or recreation lawns, lawns for shaded areas, and rough utility areas.

▬▬▬

Table 8
Wind-Tolerant and Wind-Sensitive Shrubs and Trees

Light	* requires at least 8 hours of sunlight daily;
	+ requires 4 or more hours of sunlight daily; also tolerates dappled shade;
	- tolerates less than 4 hours of sunlight daily
N.B.	Plants in more than one height category can be kept trimmed to desired height.

Wind-Tolerant

Deciduous
Up to 0.6 m
2 *   Dyer's Greenwood & Genista spp.
4 *   Brooms
4 * +   Small-Leaved Rhododendrons
5 *   Helianthemum (Rock Rose)
6 *   Spanish Gorse

Up to 1.2 m
2 *   Cinquefoil (Potentilla)
2 * +   Clavey's Dwarf Honeysuckle
6 *   Allgold Broom

Up to 2 m
2 *   Weeping Caragana
2 * +   Peking (Pointed) Cotoneaster
2 *   Golden Ninebark
4 * +   Forsythia: Northern Gold, Ottawa
5 * +   Five-Leaved Aralia
5 * +   Golden Privet
5 * + -   Mountain Laurel (Kalmia)

Up to 3 m
1 * +   Amur Maple
2 *   Caragana (Siberian Pea Shrub)
2 * +   Ninebark
2 * +   Peking (Pointed) Cotoneaster
2 *   Russian Olive
2 * +   Tatarian Honeysuckle
2 *   Common Lilac
3 * +   Common Sea Buckthorn

3 * + -   Elderberry
3 * +   Japanese Tree Lilac
3 *   Tamarix: Feathery, 5-Stamen
3 * +   Amelanchier
3 * +   Mock Orange: Sweet, Virginal
4 * +   Privets
5 * +   Cornelian Cherry *(Cornus mas)*
5 * +   Forsythia: upright, weeping

Up to 6 m
2 * +   Amur Maple
2 *   Bird (Pin) Cherry
2 *   Caragana (Siberian Pea Shrub)
2 *   Choke Cherry *(P. virginiana)*
2 *   Russian Olive
3 * +   Japanese Tree Lilac
3 * +   Amelanchier
5 *   Bradford Callery Pear
5 * +   Cornelian Cherry *(Cornus mas)*

Up to 15 m
3 *   Little Leaf Linden
3 *   Siberian Pear
6 *   Beech: Copper, Spaeth Purple
6 *   European Hornbeam
6 *   Zelkova

15 m or More
2 *   Berlin Poplar, others
2 *   Green Ash
2 * +   Sycamore Maple, others
3 *   White Willow
4 * +   Ginkgo

TABLE 8 • 171

Evergreen

1 *   White Spruce
2 *   Balsam Fir - tolerates
       moderate wind
2 *   Colorado Blue Spruce
2 *   Pine
3 * + White Cedar - tolerates
       moderate wind
3 *   Juniper - once established,
       especially *J.virginiana*
4 * + - Yew - once established

Wind-Sensitive Shrubs and Trees

American Hornbeam
Azalea
Black Locust
Boxwood *(Buxus)*
Burkwood Viburnum
Catalpa
Compact Lemoine Deutzia
Double Flowering Almond
Drooping Leucothoe
Eastern Redbud *(Cercis)*
Enkianthus
Euonymus fortunei
False Cypress *(Chamaecyparis)*
Fir—tolerates moderate wind
Flowering Almond
Golden Chain Tree *(Laburnum)*
Hemlock *(Tsuga)*
Holly
Hydrangea
Japanese Maple
Korean Spice Viburnum
Kwanzan Cherry
Larch (Tamarack)
Magnolia
Mahonia
Pieris
Pyracantha (Firethorn)
Rhododendron
Rose of Sharon *(Hibiscus)*
Wintercreeper

▨▨▨▨

Table 9
Salt-Tolerant and Salt-Sensitive Shrubs and Trees

Light   *   requires at least 8 hours of sunlight daily;

              + requires 4 or more hours of sunlight daily and tolerates dappled shade;

              - tolerates less than 4 hours of sunlight daily

Salt-Tolerant

Deciduous, up to 0.6 m
4	*	Brooms
4	* +	Cotoneasters
4	* +	Spirea: Little Princess, Bullata, Nana
5	*	Helianthemum (Rock Rose)
5	*	Lavender
6	* +	Rosemary

Evergreen, up to 0.6 m
1	* +	Bearberry *(Arctostaphylos)*
3	*	Iberis (Evergreen Candytuft)
3	*	*Juniperus horizontalis* varieties
4	* +	Cliff Green *(Pachystima)*
5	*	Heaths and Heathers

Deciduous, up to 1.2 m
2	* +	Anthony Waterer Spirea
2	*	Cinquefoil (Potentilla)
3	* + -	Alpine (Flowering) Currant
3	* + -	Annabelle Hydrangea
5	*	Broom: Allgold, other varieties
5	*	Japanese Quince
6	* +	Hydrangea: Bigleaf, Lacecap

Evergreen, up to 1.2 m
1	*	Mugo Pine
2	*	*Juniperus chinensis* varieties and cultivars
3	*	Yucca
4	*	Junipers
5	+ -	Mahonia
5	* + -	*Euonymus fortunei,* groundcovers

Deciduous, up to 2 m
2	* +	Dogwood: Red Osier, Yellowtwig
2	* +	Cotoneasters
3	* + -	Alpine (Flowering) Currant
3	* +	Bayberry
3	* +	Rugosa Roses
4	* +	Forsythia: Ottawa, Northern Gold
5	*	Butterfly Bush
5	*	Flowering Quince
5	*	Golden Privet

Deciduous, up to 3 m
2	*	Caragana (Siberean Pea Shrub)
2	*	Russian Olive
2	* +	Honeysuckle: shrub, vine
3	* +	Common Sea Buckthorn
3	*	Tamarix
4	*	Amur (Lover's) Privet
5	* +	Forsythia: upright, weeping

Deciduous Trees
2	* +	Poplar: White, Gray, Silver
2	*	Russian Olive
3	* +	European Mountain Ash
3	* +	Mulberry
3	*	White Ash
3	*	Siberian Pear
3	*	Sumac
4	* +	Ginkgo (Maidenhair Tree)
4	* +	Horse Chestnuts
4	*	Honey Locust
4	*	Willows
5	*	Apricot
5	*	Bradford Callery Pear
5	* +	Sycamore Maple

TABLE 9 • 173

Evergreen Trees

2 * Colorado Spruce
2 * Jack Pine
3 * Eastern Red Cedar
      (Juniperus virginiana)
3 * European Larch
3 * + - Yew (may require pruning)
4 * Pines: Austrian, Red, Scots
4 * + False Cypress
      (Chamaecyparis pisifera,
      C. hinoki, C. nootkatensis)

Vines

3 * + - Virginia Creeper
5 * + - Climbing Hydrangea
6 * + - English Ivy

Salt Tolerant - Many shrubs can tolerate ocean spray and a little saltiness from streets, but not drenching by slushy street salt. In this situation, protect plants with burlap barriers, and rinse plants and soil thoroughly with plenty of water in spring.

Salt-Sensitive Shrubs and Trees

Deciduous and Evergreen

Alder
American Beech
American Hornbeam
Azalea
Balsam Fir
Burning Bush (Winged Euonymus)
Canadian (Eastern) Hemlock
Crabapple
Deutzia
Dogwoods
Eastern Redbud (Cercis)
Elderberry
Flowering Almond
Flowering Dogwoods
Hackberry
Hazelnut
Hornbeam
Juniper: upright species, vars.
Larch
Linden: American, Little-Leaf
Lombardy Poplar
Maple
Mountain Laurel (Kalmia)
Oak: Pin, Red, White
Pieris
Pines: Eastern White, Japanese Red,
      Swiss Stone
Rhododendron
Rose: except rugosa
Shagbark Hickory
Snowberry (Waxberry, Symphoricarpos)
Spireas: spring blooming
Tulip Tree
Viburnum
White Spruce

▬▬▬▬▬

Table 10

Plants that Tolerate Poor, Sandy, Dry and/or Clay Conditions

Light * requires at least 8 hours of sunlight daily;
+ requires 4 or more hours of sunlight daily; also tolerates dappled shade;
- tolerates less than 4 hours of sunlight daily

zone	light		poor	sandy	dry	clay
Deciduous, up to 0.6 m						
2	*	Dyer's Greenwood, other Genista spp.	x	x	x	
4	*	Bean's Broom, other Cytisus species	x	x	x	
4	* +	*Cotoneaster adpressus*	x	x	x	
4	* +	Spirea: Little Princess, Bullata, Nana			x	x
5	* +	*Cotoneaster apiculatus* (Cranberry)	x	x	x	
5	* +	*Cotoneaster horizontalis* (Rockspray)	x	x	x	
5	*	Helianthemum (Rock Rose)	x		x	
5	*	Lavender	x		x	
5	*	Purple Broom	x	x	x	
5	*	Sage			x	
6	* +	Rosemary	x		x	
6	*	Spanish Gorse (Broom)	x	x	x	
6	* +	St. John's Wort	x	x	x	x
Evergreen, up to 0.6 m						
1	* +	Bearberry *(Arctostaphylos)*	x	x	x	
2	*	Juniper: creeping, mounding vars.	x		x	
3	*	Iberis (Evergreen Candytuft)	x			
3	+ -	Japanese Spurge (Pachysandra)			x	
3	* + -	*Vinca minor* (Periwinkle)	x			
4	* +	*Cotoneaster dammeri* (Bearberry)	x	x	x	
4	* +	Wintergreen (Teaberry)		x	x	
5	* +	*Cotoneaster dammeri* 'Coral Beauty'	x	x	x	
5	* + -	Wintercreeper - once established			x	
Deciduous, up to 1.2 m						
2	* + -	Alpine (Flowering) Currant	x		x	x
2	* +	Arctic (Basket) Willow				x
2	* +	Anthony Waterer Spirea			x	x

TABLE 10 • 175

zone	light		poor	sandy	dry	clay
2	*	Cinquefoil (Potentilla)			x	x
2	*	Dwarf Korean Lilac			x	
3	* +	Troost Birch	x			
3,4	*	Shrub Roses				x
3	* +	Spirea: Goldflame, Goldmound			x	x
4	* +	Snowbelle Mock Orange			x	x
5	*	Japanese Quince (C. japonica)			x	x
6	*	Broom: Allgold, other varieties		x	x	

Evergreen, up to 1.2 m

zone	light		poor	sandy	dry	clay
1	*	Dwarf Mugo Pine	x	x	x	
2	*	Juniper: arching, spreading vars.	x		x	
3,4	*	Yucca		x	x	
5	+ -	Mahonia		x	x	x
5	* + -	Euonymus - once established			x	

Deciduous, up to 2 m

zone	light		poor	sandy	dry	clay
2	* + -	Alpine (Flowering) Currant	x		x	x
2	*	Caragana: Weeping, Pygmy	x		x	
2	*	Dwarf Korean Lilac			x	
2,3	*	Rose: Rugosa, Harison's, Aust. Copper			x	x
2	* + -	Snowberry (Waxball)	x		x	x
3	* +	Bayberry	x		x	
	* +	Purity Mock Orange			x	x
3,4	*	Dwarf Flowering Crabapples	x		x	
3,4	*	Shrub Roses				x

Deciduous, up to 2 m

zone	light		poor	sandy	dry	clay
3	* +	Spirea: Garland, Bridal Wreath			x	x
4	* +	Cotoneaster salicifolius	x	x	x	
4	* +	Forsythia: Ottawa, Northern Gold				x
4	* + -	Kerria	x	x		
4	* +	Mock Orange: Buckley's, Minnesota			x	x
4	* +	Morrow Honeysuckle	x	x	x	
4	* +	Spirea: Snowmound, Pink			x	x
5	* +	Flowering Quince (C. speciosa)			x	x
5	*	Golden Privet		x	x	

zone	light		poor	sandy	dry	clay
Evergreen, up to 2 m						
1	*	Pumilio Mugo Pine	x	x	x	
2	*	Juniper: semi-upright varieties	x		x	
6	* +	Pyracantha (Firethorn)				x
Deciduous, up to 3 m						
2	*	Russian Olive	x	x	x	
2	* +	Tatarian Honeysuckle	x	x	x	
3	*	Common Sea Buckthorn		x	x	
3	* +	Japanese Tree Lilac			x	
2,3	*	Lilac: Common, Late, Persian			x	
3	*	Purple-Leaf Sandcherry			x	
3	*	Tamarix: 5-Stamen, Feathery		x	x	
3,4	* +	Mock Orange: Sweet, Virginal			x	x
3,4	*	Shrub Roses				x
4,5	*	Privets		x	x	
5	* +	Beauty Bush (*Kolkwitzia*)		x	x	
5	* +	Corkscrew Hazel				x
5	* +	Forsythia: upright, weeping				x
5	*	Smoke Tree	x		x	x
Evergreen, up to 3 m						
2	*	Bristlecone Pine	x	x	x	
3	*	Dwarf Scots Pine	x	x	x	
4	*	Upright Junipers	x		x	
Deciduous, up to 6 m						
2	*	Amur Maple			x	
2	*	Bird (Pin) Cherry		x		
2	*	Caragana (Siberian Pea Shrub)	x		x	
2	*	Russian Olive	x	x	x	
2	* +	Young's Weeping Birch	x			
3	+ -	American Hornbeam			x	
3	* +	American Mountain Ash				x
3	* +	Grey (Wire) Birch	x	x	x	
3	* +	Japanese Tree Lilac			x	
3	* +	Mulberry	x		x	
3	*	Purple-Leaf Sandcherry			x	

TABLE 10 • 177

zone	light		poor	sandy	dry	clay
3	* +	Ohio Buckeye			X	X
3	*	Sumac: Chinese, Dissecta, Staghorn	X		X	
3,4	* +	Amelanchier			X	
3,4	*	Flowering Crabapples	X		X	
	*	Cockspur Hawthorn			X	X
4	*	Hawthorns				X
5	* +	Angelica (Devil's Walking Stick)	X			
5	*	Bradford Callery Pear			X	
5	*	Umbrella Catalpa	X		X	
5	* +	Eastern Redbud (Cercis)			X	
5	*	Smoke Tree	X		X	X
6	*	Chinese Chestnut			X	
6	*	Goldenrain Tree (Koelreuteria)			X	

Evergreen, up to 6 m

2	*	Swiss Stone Pine	X	X	X	
2,5	*	Juniper: upright varieties	X		X	

Deciduous, up to 15 m

2	* +	Cutleaf Weeping Birch	X		X	
3	*	European Mountain Ash (Rowan)			X	X
3	*	Siberian Pear			X	
4	*	Honey Locust			X	X
4	* +	Ruby Horse Chestnut		X		X
5	*	Kentucky Coffee Tree			X	

Evergreen, up to 15 m

2	*	Pine - Jack, Scots and White	X	X	X	
3	* +	White Cedar (Thuja) - once established			X	
4	*	Pine - Austrian	X	X	X	

Deciduous, 15 m or More

1	* +	Paper (Canoe, White) Birch	X	X		
1	* +	Silver (European White) Birch	X			
2	*	Green Ash			X	
2	*	Poplars	X		X	X
2	* +	River (Silver, White) Maple			X	
3	*	Black Walnut			X	
3	*	Hackberry	X		X	

zone	light		poor	sandy	dry	clay
3	*	Red Oak		x	x	
3	*	White Ash				x
3	*	Willow				x
4	*	Black Locust	x		x	
4	* +	Horse Chestnut				x
4	*	Pin Oak			x	
5	*	Northern Catalpa			x	x
5	* +	Norway Maple			x	x

Evergreen, 15 m or More

1	*	White Spruce			x	x
2	*	Colorado Spruce			x	x
3	*	Eastern Red Cedar *(J.virginiana)*	x		x	

Vines

2	*	Honeysuckle: Dropmore Scarlet, Trumpet			x	
3	* + -	Virginia Creeper			x	
4	* +	Silver Lace Vine			x	
5	* + -	Boston Ivy			x	
5	* + -	Climbing Hydrangea			x	
5	*	Trumpet Vine *(Campsis)*			x	

TABLE 11 • 179

Table 11

pH Levels for Shrubs & Trees, Flowers, Fruits & Vegetables

N.B. Where plants are listed more than once, use the pH closest to the existing soil pH. Most plants are tolerant of a wide pH range, and it is best to adjust pH as little as possible. An all-purpose pH to aim for (except for acid loving plants) is 6.5, or within the range 6.3 to 6.7.

Soil pH for Shrubs and Trees

Alkaline, pH over 7
Cedar *(Thuja)*
Butterfly Bush
Clematis
Euonymus
Flowering Almond
Forsythia
Helianthemum (Rock Rose)
Honeysuckle
Hornbeam
Ilex (Holly)
Juniper
Lavender
Lilac
Potentilla (Cinquefoil)
Quince *(Chaenomeles)*
Red Osier Dogwood
Rosemary
Rowan (European Mountain Ash)
Russian Olive
Scots Pine
Smoke Tree
Snowberry (Waxberry)
White Pine
Wisteria
Yew

Neutral, pH 6 1/2 to 7
Apple
Apricot
Beech
Box
Cedar *(Thuja)*
Cotoneaster

Crabapple
Crataegus
Currant
Deutzia
Elderberry
Euonymus
Firethorn (Pyracantha)
Flowering Almond
Forsythia
Ginkgo
Grass
Hawthorn
Hibiscus
Hornbeam
Hydrangea - acid for blue flowers
Ilex (Holly)
Juniper
Larch
Lilac
Linden
Locust
Maple
Mock Orange
Mulberry
Privet
Prunus
Quince *(Chaenomeles)*
Rose
Russian Olive
Spirea
St. John's Wort
Tamarix
Tulip Tree
Viburnum

Vinca minor (Periwinkle)
Weigela
Witch Hazel
Willow
Yew

Acid, pH 5 1/2 to 6
Amelanchier
Birch
Bradford Callery Pear
Broom
Chamaecyparis
Cliff Green *(Pachystima)*
Cotoneaster
Daphne
Dogwood
Fir
Flowering Cherry
Gaultheria (Wintergreen)
Gooseberry
Grape
Heath, Heather
Hemlock
Juniper

Kerria
Leucothoe
Magnolia
Mahonia
Mayflower
Mountain Laurel (Kalmia)
Oak
Pachysandra
Pieris
Pine
Plum
Raspberry
Spruce
St. John's Wort
Vaccinium

Very Acid, pH 5 or less
Aspen
Azalea
Bayberry
Bueberry
Rhododendron

TABLE 11 • 181

Soil pH for Flowers

Alkaline, pH over 7

Anemone
Aster
Aubrieta
Calendula
Campanula
Dahlia
Dianthus
Geranium
Helianthemum (Rock Rose)
Hollyhock
Iris
Lilium candidum
Mignonette
Mimosa
Morning Glories
Nasturtium
Pansy
Petunia
Phlox
Salvia
Snapdragon
Sweet Pea
Tulip
Verbena
Viola

Hepatica
Hibiscus
Iris
Lavender
Lilium candidum
Lobelia
Lupine
Marigold
Narcissus
Nymphaea (Water Lily)
Ornithogalum
Oxalis
Passion Flower
Peony
Poinsetta
Poppy
Primula
Rose

Neutral, pH 6 1/2 to 7

Agapanthus
Ageratum
Alyssum
Anemone
Carnation
Coleus
Columbine
Centurea
Chrysthemum
Cosmos
Crocus
Delphinium
Fuchsia
Gladiolus
Helleborus

Acid, pH 5 1/2 to 6

Amaryllis
Begonia
Bleeding Heart
Bloodroot
Camellia
Citrus
Cyclamen
Ferns
Gardenia
Lilium: most species
Magnolia
Phlox

Very Acid—pH 5 or less

Orchid

Soil pH for Fruits and Vegetables

Alkaline, pH over 7
Alfalfa
Asparagus
Cabbage
Carrot
Cauliflower
Celery
Clover
Lettuce
Parsley
Wheat

Neutral, pH 6 1/2 to 7
Beet
Broccoli
Buckwheat
Chives
Corn
Cucumber
Currant
Eggplant
Elderberry
Endive
Melon
Mulberry
Onion
Passion Fruit
Pea
Plum
Radish
Rhubarb
Soybean
Spinach

Acid - pH 5 1/2 to 6
Amelanchier
Bean
Blackberry
Gooseberry
Grape
Oats
Parsnip
Pepper
Plum
Potato
Pumpkin
Raspberry
Rutabaga
Rye
Squash
Strawberry
Sweet Potato
Tomato
Turnip

Very Acid - pH 5 or less
Blueberry
Watermelon

TABLE 12 • 183

Table 12

Shrubs and Trees Tolerating Wet Conditions

Light   * requires at least 8 hours of sunlight daily;
       + requires 4 or more hours of sunlight daily and tolerates dappled shade;
       - tolerates less than 4 hours of sunlight daily

Deciduous, up to 0.6 m
2   * + -Dwarf Birch *(B. michauxii)*

Evergreen - up to 0.6 m
1   * +   Bog LaureL *(K. polifolia)*
2   * +   Lambkill *(K. angustifolia)*
2   * +   Bog Rosemary, Andromeda

Deciduous, up to 1.2 m
2   * +   Arctic (Basket) Willow
4   * +   Red Chokeberry
5   *   Japanese Quince

Evergreen, up to 1.2 m
3   *   Wild Rhododendron
3   +   Leatherleaf *(Chamaedaphne)*
5   * + -Euonymus

Deciduous, up to 2 m
2   * +   Red Osier Dogwood
2   * +   Swamp Birch *(B. pumila)*
3   * +   Bayberry
3   * +   Canada Holly *(Ilex verticillata)*
3   +   Wild Holly *(Nemopanthus mucronatus)*
5   * +   Siberian Dogwood
5   *   Flowering Quince

Deciduous, up to 3 m
2   * +   Highbush Cranberry
2   * +   Nannyberry
3   * + -Elderberry (some wetness)
5   * +   Corkscrew Hazel

Deciduous, up to 6 m
2   * +   Common Witch Hazel
2   * +   Nannyberry
2   * +   (European) Snowball Viburnum
3   + -   American Hornbeam
3   * +   Gray Birch
4   + -   Alternate-Leaf Dogwood
5   *   Bradford Callery Pear

Deciduous, up to 15 m
3   *   Siberian Pear
5   *   Trumpet Vine *(Campsis)*

Evergreen, up to 15 m
3   * +   American Larch (Tamarack)
3   * +   White Cedar *(Thuja)*
6   * +   Weeping Nootka False Cypress

Deciduous, 15 m or more
2   *   Poplars
3   * +   Red Maple
3   *   White Willow
4   * +   Black (Red, River) Birch
4   *   Pin Oak

Evergreen, 15 m or more
2   *   Balsam Fir
3   * +   European Larch *(L. decidua)*
4   * +   Canadian (Eastern) Hemlock

Larches are deciduous, but are similar to coniferous evergreens in shape and function.

Table 13

Deciduous Plants Resistant to, or Tolerant of, Pests or Disease

Light * requires at least 8 hours of sunlight daily;
+ rquires 4 or more hours of sunlight daily; also tolerates dappled shade;
- tolerates less than 4 hours of sunlight daily

zone	light		insect	disease
Up to 0.6 m				
4,5	*	Brooms	x	
3,4	*	Shrub Rose: Red Max Graf, Henry Hudson, rugosa repens rosea		x
Up to 1.2 m				
2	*	Cinquefoil (Potentilla)	x	
3,4	*	Shrub Rose: Champlain, Robusta, Thompson, Dart's Dash		x
4	* +	Red Chokeberry	x	
6	*	Allgold Broom and varieties	x	x
Up to 2 m				
2	* +	Yellowedge Dogwood	x	x
3,4	*	Shrub Roses: Hansa, Jens Munk, Martin Frobisher, Therese Bugnet, Morden Ruby, Pink Surprise, Alexander MacKenzie, John Davis		x
4	* +	Morrow Honeysuckle	x	x
5	* +	Siberian Dogwood	x	x
5	* + -	Five-Leaved Aralia	x	
Up to 3 m				
2	* +	Tatarian Honeysuckle	x	x
3,4	*	Shrub Roses: William Baffin, John Cabot, Henry Kelsey		x
4	*	Ibolium Privet		x
Up to 6 m				
2	* +	Amur Maple	x	
2	*	Russian Olive	x	
3	* + -	Hop-Hornbeam (Ironwood)	x	x
3	* +	Ohio Buckeye - some resistance to blight		x
3,4	* +	Amelanchier	x	
4	+-	Alternate-Leaf Dogwood	x	x

TABLE 13 • 185

zone	light		insect	disease
5	*	Bradford Callery Pear - resists fireblight		x
5	* +	Cornelian Cherry *(Cornus mas)*	x	x
6	* +	Golden Chain Tree *(Laburnum)*		x
6	+ -	Japanese Maple	x	x

Up to 15 m

zone	light		insect	disease
3	*	Amur Cork Tree	x	x
3	*	Siberian Pear - resists fireblight		x
4	*	Honey-Locust		x
5	*	Kentucky Coffee Tree	x	x
6	*	Zelkova		x

15 m or More

zone	light		insect	disease
2	*	Green Ash	x	x
2	* +	River (Silver, White) Maple		x
3	*	Hackberry	x	x
4	* + -	Ginkgo (Maidenhair Tree)	x	x
5	*	English Oak		x
5	* +	Norway Maple	x	
5	* +	Catalpa		x
5	*	Tulip Tree		x

Vines

zone	light		insect	disease
2,4	*	Honeysuckle Vines	x	x

Table 14

Shrubs, Trees and Vines Suitable for Growing in Containers

Light * requires at least 8 hours of sunlight daily ;
+ requires 4 or more hours of sunlight daily and tolerates dappled shade;
- tolerates less than 4 hours of sunlight daily

zone	light	

Deciduous, up to 0.6 m

4	* +	*Cotoneaster adpressus* (Creeping)
4	* +	Spirea: Little Princess, Bullata
5	* +	*Cotoneaster horizontalis* (Rockspray)
5	*	Helianthemum (Rock Rose)
5	*	Lavender
5	*	Sage
6	*	Rosemary
6	* +	St. John's Wort

Broad-Leaved Evergreens, up to 0.6 m

3	*	Garland Flower *(Daphne cneorum)*
4	* +	*Cotoneaster dammeri* (Bearberry)
4	* +	Small-Leaved Rhododendrons
4,5	*	Heaths, Heathers
5	* +	*Cotoneaster dammeri* 'Coral Beauty'
5	* + -	Euonymus
5,6	* + -	Box: Pincushion, Green Gem

Deciduous, up to 1.2 m

2,3	* +	Spirea: Anthony Waterer, Goldflame, Goldmound
2	* +	Cinquefoil (Potentilla)
2	*	Dwarf Korean Lilac
3	* + -	Annabelle Hydrangeaa
3	* +	Dwarf Burning Bush
3	* +	February Daphne *(Daphne mezereum)*
3	* +	Troost Birch
4	* +	Snowbelle Mock Orange
5	+	Burkwood Daphne
5	*	Japanese Quince *(C.japonica)*
6	* +	Hydrangea: Bigleaf, Lacecap, Oakleaf

TABLE 14 • 187

zone   light

Broad-Leaved Evergreens, up to 1.2 m
3,4	*	Yucca: Spanish Bayonet, Adam's Needle
4,5	* +	Rhododendrons
5	+ -	Mahonia
5	* + -	Winter Beauty Korean Box
6	* +	Azalea: Kurume, Kaempferi
6	+	Drooping Leucothoe

Deciduous, up to 2 m
2	* + -	Snowberry (Waxball)
2	*	Weeping Caragana
3,4	*	Dwarf Flowering Crabapple
3,4	* +	Mock Orange: Purity, Snowflake, Buckley's Quill
3,4	* +	Spirea: Garland, Bridal Wreath
4,6	*	Roses: small shrubs, floribundas, polyanthas and miniatures.
5	* +	Azaleas
5	*	Common (Flowering) Quince (C.speciosa)
5	* + -	Kerria
5	* +	Viburnum: Burkwood, Korean Spice
6	*	Hibiscus syriacus (Rose of Sharon)

Broad-Leaved Evergreens, up to 2 m
5	* + -	Tall Boy Box
5,6	+	Pieris floribunda, Pieris japonica
5,6	* +	Rhododendrons
6	* +	Firethorn (Pyracantha)
6	* +	Hollies

Deciduous, up to 3 m
2	*	Caragana (Siberian Pea Shrub)
2	* +	Tatarian Honeysuckle
2,3	*	Common Lilac
3,4	* +	Mock Orange: Sweet,Virginal
4	*	Privet
4,5	* +	Spirea: Snowmound, Pink
5	* +	Forsythia: upright, weeping
5	*	Beauty Bush (Kolkwitzia)
5	*	Smoke Tree
5	*	Star Magnolia (keep moist)
6	*	Eastern Redbud (Cercis)
6	+ -	Japanese Maple (keep moist)

zone   light

Deciduous, up to 6 m

2	* +	Amur Maple
2	* +	Birch: Young's Weeping, Cutleaf Weeping
2	*	Russian Olive
3	*	Purple-Leaf Sandcherry
3	*	Sumac 'Dissecta' ('Laciniata')
3,4	* +	Amelanchier
3,4	*	Flowering Crabapples, especially Red Jade
4	+ -	Alternate-Leaf Dogwood
4	*	Hawthorns
5	*	Bradford Callery Pear
5	* +	Chinese Flowering Dogwood
5	*	Fringetree *(Chionanthus)*
6	*	Beech: Weeping Purple, Copper, Spaeth Purple
6	*	Japanese Cherry: Kwanzan, Weeping
6	*	Goldenrain Tree *(Koelreuteria)*
6	*	Golden Chain Tree *(Laburnum)*
6	+ -	Japanese Maple

Deciduous, small shade trees

2	*	Green Ash
3	*	European Mountain Ash (Rowan)
4	* +	Ginkgo (Maidenhair Tree)
4	*	Honey-Locust: Shademaster, Skyline, Sunburst
4	*	Pin Oak
4	*	Black Locust
6	*	Zelkova

Vines

4,5	* +	Clematis hybrids (species are too vigorous)
5	* + -	Wintercreeper
5	*	Wisteria (train to single trunk)
6	+ -	English Ivy 'Baltica'

Tender Plants (Winter Indoors), up to 3 m

T	* +	Bayleaf
T	* +	Bougainvillea
T	* +	Camellia
T	* +	Gardenia
T	* +	*Hibiscus rosa-sinensis* (houseplant)
T	* +	Jasmine

Coniferous Evergreens

Most coniferous evergreens are suitable, ranging from dwarf varieties to tall, upright plants. Hemlock and False Cypress *(Chamaecyparis)* are very difficult because they must be kept evenly moist.

TABLE 15 • 189

Table 15

Sequence of Colours —bulbs, perennials, shrubs, trees, vines

	white	pink	rose	red	orange	yellow	cream	blue	mauve	purple
EARLY SPRING										
Bulbs										
Bulbous Iris	white					yellow		blue		purple
Chiondoxa		pink						blue		
Crocus	white					yellow			mauve	purple
Eranthis						yellow				
Miniature Daffodils						yellow	cream			
Siberian Squill								blue		
Snowdrop	white									
Tulip species			rose	red		yellow				
Perennials										
Arabis	white	pink								
Arenaria	white									
Aubrieta									mauve	purple
Cerastium	white									
Cyclamen		pink		red						
Doronicum						yellow				
Draba						yellow				
Forget-me-not								blue		
Iberis	white									
Phlox,creeping	white	pink							mauve	
Polemonium								blue		
Primula	white		rose		orange	yellow			mauve	purple
Pulmonaria		pink						blue		
Violets	white							blue	mauve	purple
Shrubs, Trees										
Amelanchier	white									
Cornelian Cherry						yellow				
Daphne			rose							purple
Erica, Heaths	white	pink	rose						mauve	purple
Flowering Quince				red	orange					
Forsythia						yellow				

	white	pink	rose	red	orange	yellow	cream	blue	mauve	purple
Japanese Quince				red	orange					
Kerria						yellow				
Magnolia: star	white									
Magnolia: saucer		pink								
Mahonia						yellow				
Rhododendron	white	pink		red		yellow			mauve	purple

LATE SPRING

Bulbs

	white	pink	rose	red	orange	yellow	cream	blue	mauve	purple
Allium	white		rose			yellow			mauve	purple
Anemone blanda	white	pink		red				blue		
Crown Imperial					orange	yellow				
Daffodils	white					yellow	cream			
Dogtooth Violet	white	pink	rose			yellow				purple
Grape Hyacinth								blue		purple
Hyacinth	white	pink	rose		orange	yellow		blue	mauve	purple
Puschkinia								blue		
Snakeshead Fritillary										purple
Snowflake	white									
Tulips	white	pink	rose	red	orange	yellow	cream		mauve	purple
Wood Hyacinth	white	pink						blue		

Perennials

	white	pink	rose	red	orange	yellow	cream	blue	mauve	purple
Ajuga								blue		
Alyssum						yellow				
Aquilegia	white			red		yellow		blue	mauve	purple
Arabis	white	pink								
Arenaria	white									
Armeria		pink								
Aubrieta									mauve	purple
Baby's Breath	white	pink								
Bellis (English Daisy)	white	pink		red						
Bleeding Hearts	white	pink								
Bog Rosemary	white	pink								
Camassia								blue		
Cerastium	white									
Coralbells	white	pink		red						
Cranesbill		pink						blue		

TABLE 15 • 191

	white	pink	rose	red	orange	yellow	cream	blue	mauve	purple
Daylilies		pink	rose	red	orange	yellow	cream			purple
Dianthus	white	pink		red						
Doronicum						yellow				
Geum					orange	yellow				
Helleborus	white									
Iris: Pumila	white		rose	red	orange	yellow		blue	mauve	purple
Lunaria (Honesty)	white									purple
Lupines		pink		red		yellow		blue	purple	
Lychnis		pink								
Meadowsweet	white									
Pansies	white			red		yellow		blue	mauve	purple
Penstemon				red				blue		purple
Poppies	white	pink		red	orange	yellow				
Potentilla	white	pink		red		yellow				
Primula	white	pink	rose	red	orange	yellow	cream			purple
Saxifrage	white	pink				yellow				purple
Sedum		pink				yellow				
Sempervivum		pink				yellow				
St. John's Wort						yellow				
Thyme, Creeping	white								mauve	purple
Trillium	white	pink		red						
Trollius (Globeflower)					orange	yellow				
Valerian	white	pink								
Virginia Bluebells								blue		

Shrubs, Trees, Vines

	white	pink	rose	red	orange	yellow	cream	blue	mauve	purple
Apple, Crabapple	white	pink		red						
Azalea	white	pink		red	orange	yellow	cream		mauve	purple
Beauty Bush		pink								
Cercis (Redbud)		pink								
Chinese Fl. Dogwood	white									
Clematis	white	pink		red				blue		purple
Cotoneaster	white	pink								
Cytisus (Broom)				red		yellow				
Deutzia	white									
Enkianthus	white									

	white	pink	rose	red	orange	yellow	cream	blue	mauve	purple
Erica, Heaths	white	pink	rose						mauve	purple
Five-Leaf Akebia										purple
Flowering Almond	white	pink								
Hawthorns	white	pink		red						
Iberis	white	pink								
Laburnum						yellow				
Leucothoe	white									
Lilac	white		rose					blue	mauve	purple
Magnolia: Oyama	white									
Mountain Laurel	white	pink		red						
Pieris	white									
Purple-Leaf Sandcherry	white	pink								
Rhododendron	white		rose	red					mauve	purple
Spirea: Garland	white									
Tamarix: Feathery		pink								
Viburnums	white									
Vinca minor	white							blue		purple
Weigela	white	pink		red						
Wisteria	white	pink						blue		purple

SUMMER

Tender Bulbs   High maintenance. Store indoors over winter.

	white	pink	rose	red	orange	yellow	cream	blue	mauve	purple
Acidanthera	white									
Anemone coronaria	white	pink		red				blue	mauve	
Begonia	white	pink		red	orange	yellow				
Caladium	white	pink		red						
Calla Lily	white	pink				yellow				
Canna	white	pink		red		yellow				
Dahlia	white	pink		red	orange	yellow	cream		mauve	purple
Gladiolus	white	pink	rose	red	orange	yellow	cream		mauve	purple
Ismene	white					yellow				
Montbretia					orange	yellow				
Oxalis	white	pink	rose							
Ranunculus	white			red	orange	yellow				
Tigridia	white			red	orange	yellow				
Tuberose	white									

TABLE 15 • 193

	white	pink	rose	red	orange	yellow	cream	blue	mauve	purple

Perennials

	white	pink	rose	red	orange	yellow	cream	blue	mauve	purple
Achillea	white					yellow				
Aruncus	white									
Astilbe	white	pink	rose	red					mauve	
Baby's Breath	white									
Beebalm (Monarda)	white	pink		red						
Butterfly Weed					orange					
Campanula	white							blue		
Carnation	white	pink		red						
Centaurea								blue		
Coralbells	white	pink		red						
Coreopsis						yellow				
Cranesbill		pink						blue		
Cynoglossum								blue		
Daylilies		pink	rose	red	orange	yellow	cream			purple
Delphinium								blue		
Dianthus	white	pink		red						
Evening Primrose						yellow				
Feverfew	white									
Foxglove	white	pink	rose				cream			
Gaillardia				red	orange	yellow				
Gasplant	white	pink								
Gazania				red	orange	yellow	cream			
Hollyhock		pink	rose		orange	yellow	cream			
Hosta	white							blue		purple
Iris: Japanese	white	pink	rose					blue	mauve	purple
Iris: Bearded, Siberian	white	pink	rose	red	orange	yellow	cream	blue	mauve	purple
Lavatera (Mallow)	white	pink		red						
Lavender									mauve	purple
Liatris	white								mauve	purple
Lilies	white	pink	rose	red	orange	yellow	cream			
Lily-of-the-Valley	white									
Lychnis		pink								
Monkshood									mauve	purple
Pansies	white			red		yellow		blue	mauve	purple

	white	pink	rose	red	orange	yellow	cream	blue	mauve	purple
Penstemon				red				blue		purple
Peony	white	pink		red						
Phlox	white	pink		red				blue		
Sedum		pink	rose							
Shasta Daisy	white									
Veronica	white							blue	mauve	purple
Yucca	white									

Shrubs, Trees, Vines

	white	pink	rose	red	orange	yellow	cream	blue	mauve	purple
Black Locust	white									
Butterfly Bush	white							blue	mauve	purple
Clematis	white	pink		red				blue	mauve	purple
Climbing Hydrangea	white									
Elderberry	white									
False Spirea	white									
Fringetree	white									
Heaths, Heathers	white	pink	rose						mauve	purple
Helianthemum		pink	rose				cream			
Hibiscus syriacus	white	pink	rose							purple
Honeysuckle	white	pink		red						
Magnolia: Oyama	white									
Mock Orange	white									
Potentilla	white				orange	yellow				
Roses	white	pink	rose	red	orange	yellow	cream			purple
Spirea:BridalWreath	white									
- Goldflame, Goldmound		pink								
- Anthony Waterer			rose							
- Little Princess		pink								
St. John's Wort						yellow				
Trumpet Vine (Campsis)				red	orange	yellow				

AUTUMN

Bulbs

	white	pink	rose	red	orange	yellow	cream	blue	mauve	purple
Anemone coronaria	white	pink		red				blue	mauve	
Autumn Crocus									mauve	
Colchicum	white		rose						mauve	purple

TABLE 15 • 195

	white	pink	rose	red	orange	yellow	cream	blue	mauve	purple

Perennials

	white	pink	rose	red	orange	yellow	cream	blue	mauve	purple
Achillea	white					yellow				
Aster		pink		red		yellow		blue		purple
Baby's Breath	white									
Butterfly Weed					orange	yellow				
Campanula	white							blue		
Chrysanthemum,hardy	white	pink		red	orange	yellow				purple
Feverfew	white									
Gazania				red	orange	yellow	cream			
Goldenrod						yellow				
Hollyhock		pink	rose		orange	yellow	cream			
Hosta	white							blue		
Michaelmas Daisy		pink		red		yellow		blue		purple
Monkshood									mauve	purple
Pansies	white			red		yellow		blue		purple
Purple Coneflower				red	orange					purple
Purple Loosestrife		pink	rose	red						
Rudbeckia					orange	yellow				
Sedum		pink	rose							

Shrubs, Trees, Vines

	white	pink	rose	red	orange	yellow	cream	blue	mauve	purple
Butterfly Bush	white							blue	mauve	purple
Common Witch Hazel						yellow				
Golden Clematis						yellow				
Heaths, Heathers	white	pink	rose						mauve	purple
Hibiscus syriacus	white	pink	rose							purple
Hydrangea	white	pink						blue		
Potentilla	white				orange	yellow				
Roses	white	pink	rose	red	orange	yellow	cream			purple
Silver Lace Vine	white									
St. John's Wort						yellow				
Sweet Aut. Clematis	white									
Tamarix: Five-Stamen		pink								

Many shrubs and trees bear fruit that contribute colour in summer and autumn. Some fruits cling into winter as well, adding to the winter landscape. Fruiting shrubs and trees include, in increasing order of height:

Black
Korean Spice and
  Burkwood Viburnums
Cotoneasters
Elderberry
Wayfaring Tree

Blue
Blueberry
Witherod
Nannyberry
Amelanchier

Orange
Firethorn
Honeysuckle

Purple
Grape
Purple-Leaf Sandcherry

White
Snowberry

Yellow
Common Sea Buckthorn

Red
Cotoneasters
Shrub Roses
Currant
Hollies
Dwarf Crabapple
Burning Bush
Yew
Honeysuckle
Cornelian Cherry
Highbush Cranberry
Crabapple
Hawthorn

Soil Analysis

To take a soil sample, push a spade into the soil at several sites around the garden. At each site, collect soil from the top of the cut through to the bottom. Mix all of these in a bucket, and then take a cupful or two of that mixture to send off for analysis. Put it in a plastic bag, include your name and address, and send it to the Department of Agriculture in your province or state. Ask that the soil be analysed for pH, nutrients, and organic content, and state what crops you want to grow—lawn, flowers, fruit trees, etc.

List of Plant Names

Almond: Double Flowering, *Prunus glandulosa 'sinensis'*;
Flowering, *P. triloba 'multiplex'*
Alternate-Leaf Dogwood, *Cornus alternifolia*
Amelanchier (Serviceberry, Juneberry, Shadblow, Saskatoon,
Indian Pear), *Amenlanchier spp.*
Amur Cork Tree, *Phellodendron amurense*
Angelica, *Aralia elata*
Apple, *Malus pumila (M. domestica)*
Apricot, *Prunus armeniaca*
Ash: Green, *Fraxinus pennsylvanica*; White, *F. americana*
Azaleas, *Rhododendron spp. and hybrids*

Basswood, *Tilia americana*
Bayberry, *Myrica pensylvanica*
Bearberry, *Arctostaphylos uva-ursi*
Beauty Bush, *Kolkwitzia amabilis*
Beech: American, *Fagus grandifolia*; Blue, *Carpinus caroliniana*;
Copper, *F. sylvatica 'cuprea'*; Spaeth Purple,
F. s. 'Spaethii'; Weeping Purple, *F. s. 'purpurea-pendula'*
Birch: Black (Red, River), *Betula nigra*; Dwarf, *B. michauxii*;
Canoe (Paper), *B. papyifera*; Chinese Paper, *B. albo-sinensis*;
Common (Silver, White), *B. pendula (B. alba, B. verrucosa)*;
Cutleaf Weeping, *B. pendula 'gracilis'*; Gray (Wire), *B. pop-
ulifolia*; Himalayan, *B. utilis*; Swamp (Bog), *B. pumila*;
Troost, *B. alba 'Troost Dwarf'*; Young's Weeping, *B. pendula
'Youngii'*
Bittersweet, *Celastrus scandens or C. orbiculatus*
Black Locust, *Robinia pseudoacacia*
Blueberry: Highbush, *Vaccinium corymbosum*;
Wild, *V. angustifolium*
Bog (Swamp) Laurel, *Kalmia polifolia*
Bog Rosemary, *Andromeda polifolia*
Boston Ivy, *Parthenocissus tricuspidata*
Box: Pincushion, *Buxus microphylla koreana 'Pincushion'*; Tall
Boy, *B. m. k. 'Tall Boy'*; Winter Beauty Korean, *B. m. k.
'Winter Beauty'*

Bradford Callery Pear, *Pyrus calleryana 'Bradford'*
Broom: Allgold, *Cytisus x praecox 'Allgold'*; Bean's, *C. x beanii*;
  Dyer's Greenwood, *Genista tinctoria; Genista, G. pilosa* and
  G. sagittalis; Purple, *C. purpureus*; Spanish Gorse,
  G. hispanica
Burning Bush: Winged Euonymus, *Euonymus alatus*; Dwarf,
  E. a. 'Compacta'
Butterfly Bush, *Buddleia davidii*

Caragana: Pygmy, *Caragana pygmaea*; Siberian Pea Shrub,
  C. arborescens; Weeping, *C. a. 'Pendula'*
Catalpa: Northern, *Catalpa speciosa*; Umbrella, *C. bignonioides*
  'nana'
Cedar (Arborvitae, Cypress): Globe, *Thuja occidentalis vars.*;
  Upright, *T. occidentalis vars.*; Eastern, *see Juniper*; White,
  T. occidentalis
Cherry: Bird (Pin), *Prunus pensylvanica*; Choke, *P. virginiana*;
  Kwanzan Japanese, *P. serrulata 'Kwanzan'*; Nanking
  (Manchu), *P. tomentosa*; Purple-Leaf Sandcherry, *P. x*
  cistena; Sour, *P. cerasus*; Sweet, *P. avium*; Weeping Japanese,
  P. s. 'Kiku Shidare'
Chinese Chestnut, *Castanea mollissima*
Chokeberry: Red, *Aronia arbutifolia*
Cinquefoil, *Potentilla fruticosa vars.*
Clematis: Large-Flowered, *Clematis hybrids*; Sweet Autumn,
  C. maximowicziana; Golden (Tangutica), *C. tangutica 'aureolin'*
Cliff Green, *Pachystima canbyi (Paxistima)*
Corkscrew Hazel, *Corylus avellana 'contorta'*
Cornelian Cherry, *Cornus mas*
Cotoneaster: Bearberry, *Cotoneaster dammeri*; Coral Beauty,
  C. d. 'Coral Beauty'; Cranberry, *C. apiculatus*; Creeping,
  C. adpressus; Littleleaf, *C. microphyllus*; Peking (Pointed),
  C. acutifolius; Praecox, *C. adpressus 'Praecox'*; Rockspray,
  C. horizontalis; Salicifolius, *C. salicifolius*
Crabapple: Flowering, *Malus spp. and vars.*; Dwarf Flowering,
  Malus spp. and vars.; Red Jade, *M. x 'Red Jade'*
Cranberry: Large, *Vaccinium macrocarpon*; Small, *V. oxycoccos*
Crowberry: Black, *Empetrum nigrum*
Crown Vetch, *Coronilla varia*
Currant: Flowering (Alpine), *Ribes alpinum*; Garden, *Ribes spp.*
Cypress: Leyland, *x Cupressocyparis leylandii*
Cytisus, see Broom

Daphne: Burkwood, *Daphne x burkwoodii;* February,
  D. mezereum; Garland Flower (Rose Daphne), *D. cneorum*
Deutzia: Compact Lemoine, *Deutzia x lemoinei*
Devil's Walking Stick, *Aralia elata*
Dogwood: Alternate-Leaf, *Cornus alternifolia;* Chinese
  Flowering, *C. kousa chinensis;* Red Osier, *C. stolonifera;*
  Siberian, *C. alba 'Siberica';* Silveredge, *C. a. 'elegantissima';*
  Yellowedge (Mottled) *C. a. 'Gouchaultii';* Yellowtwig,
  C. s. 'flaviramea'
Dutchman's Pipe, *Aristolochia durior*
Eastern Redbud (Judas Tree), *Cercis canadensis*
Elderberry, *Sambucus canadensis*
Enkianthus, *Enkianthus companulatus*
Euonymus: Groundcovers, *Euonymus fortunei vars.;* Sarcoxie,
  E. f. 'Sarcoxie'; Winged, *see Burning Bush*

False Cypress: Dwarf Hinoki, *Chamaecyparis obtusa 'nana*
  gracilis'; Fernspray, *C. o. 'filicoides';* Golden Threadleaf,
  C. pisifera 'filifera aurea'; Sawara, *C. pisifera;* Threadleaf,
  C. p. 'filifera'; Weeping Nootka, *C. nootkatensis 'pendula'*
False Spirea, *Sorbaria sorbifolia*
Fir: Balsam, *Abies balsamea;* Douglas, *Pseudotsuga menziesii;*
  Dwarf Balsam, *Abies balsamea 'nana';* Dwarf Rocky
  Mountain, *A. lasiocarpa 'compacta';* Korean, *A. koreana;*
  Silver (White), *A. concolor*
Firethorn (Pyracantha), *Pyracantha coccinea*
Five-Leaf Akebia, *Akebia quinata*
Five-Leaved Aralia, *Acanthopanax sieboldianus*
Forsythia: Northern Gold, *Forsythia ovata 'Northern Gold';*
  Ottawa, *F. ovata 'Ottawa';* Upright, *F. intermedia vars.;*
  Weeping, *F. suspensa*
Foxberry, *Vaccinium vitis-idaea*
Fringetree, *Chionanthus virginicus*

Genista, see Broom
Ginkgo (Maidenhair Tree), *Ginkgo biloba*
Golden Chain Tree, *Laburnum x watereri*
Goldenrain Tree, *Koelreuteria paniculata*
Gorse, *see Broom*
Grape, *Vitis spp. and vars.*

Hackberry, *Celtis occidentalis*

Hawthorn, *Crataegus spp.*

Heath, *Erica spp.*

Heather, *Calluna vulgaris*

Helianthemum (Rock Rose), *Helianthemum nummularium*

Hemlock: Canadian (Eastern), *Tsuga canadensis;* Calvert, *T. c. 'Calvert'*; Cole's Prostrate, *T. c. 'Cole's Prostrate'*; Jeddeloh, *T. c. 'Jeddeloh'*; Pomfret, *T. c. 'Pomfret'*; Sargent Weeping, *T. c. 'pendula'*

Hibiscus: Rose of China, *Hibiscus rosa-sinensis;* Rose of Sharon, *H. syriacus*

Hickory: Shagbark, *Carya ovata*

Highbush Cranberry, *Viburnum trilobum (V. opulus)*

Hobblebush, *Viburnum alnifolium*

Holly: Canada (Winterberry), *Ilex verticillata;* Japanese, *I. crenata;* Meservae (Blue), *I. x meserveae;* Mountain (Wild), *Nemopanthus mucronatus*

Honey-Locust, *Gleditsia triacanthos*

Honeysuckle: Clavey's Dwarf, *Lonicera xylosteum 'Claveyi'*; Dropmore Scarlet, *L. x brownii;* Hall's, *L. japonica 'Halliana'*; Morrow, *L. morrowii;* Tatarian, *L. tatarica;* Trumpet, *L. sempervirens*

Hornbeam: Hop, *Ostrya virginiana;* American, *Carpinus caroliniana;* Pyramidal European, *C. betulus 'fastigiata'*

Horse Chestnut: Common, *Aesculus hippocastanum;* Ruby, *A. x carnea*

Huckleberry, *Gaylussacia baccata*

Hydrangea: Annabelle, *Hydrangea arborescens 'Annabelle'*; Bigleaf, Lacecap, *H. macrophylla (H. hortensia)*; Climbing, *H. anomala* var. *petiolaris;* Oakleaf, *H. quercifolia;* Peegee, *H. paniculata 'grandiflora'*

Iberis (Evergreen Candytuft), *Iberis sempervirens*

Ironwood (Hop Hornbeam), *Ostrya virginiana*

Ivy: Baltic, *Hedera helix 'Baltica'*; English (Common), *H. helix*

Japanese Spurge, *Pachysandra terminalis*

Jasmine, *Jasminum officinale*

Juniper: Eastern Red Cedar, *Juniperus virginiana*

Kentucky Coffee Tree, *Gymnocladus dioica*
Kerria, *Kerria japonica*
Kiwi: Hardy, *Actinidia arguta, A. kolomikta*

Labrador Tea, *Ledum groenlandicum*
Lace Shrub: Groundcover, *Stephanandra incisa 'crispa'*;
    Upright, *S. incisa*
Lambkill (Sheep's Laurel), *Kalmia angustifolia*
Lavender, *Lavandula spp.*
Leatherleaf, *Chamaedaphne calyculata*
Larch (Tamarack): American, *Larix laricina*; European,
    L. decidua
Leucothoe: Drooping, *Leucothoe fontanesiana*
Lilac: Common, Persian, Preston, *Syringa spp. and cultivars*;
    Dwarf Korean, *S. patula*; Japanese Tree, *S. reticulata*
    (S.japonica)
Linden: American, *Tilia americana*; Little-Leaf, *T. cordata*

Magnolia: Oyama, *Magnolia sieboldii*; Saucer, *M. x soulangiana*;
    Star, *M. stellata*
Mahonia (Oregon, Holly Grape), *Mahonia aquifolium*
Maple: Amur, *Acer ginnala*; Cutleaf Japanese, *A. palmatum
    'dissectum'*; Globe Norway, *A. platanoides 'globosum'*;
    Harlequin, *A. platanoides 'Drummondii'*; Japanese, *A. palma-
    tum vars.*; Mountain, *A. spicatum*; Norway, *A. platanoides*;
    Red, *A. rubrum*; River (Silver, White), *A. saccharinum (A.
    dasycarpum)*; Striped (Moose), *A. pensylvanicum*; Sycamore
    (Plane), *A. pseudoplatanus*; Sugar, *A. saccharum*
Microbiota, *Microbiota decussata*
Mock Orange: Buckley's Quill, *Philadelphus x 'Buckley's Quill'*;
    Golden, *P. coronarius 'aureus'*; Purity, *P. x virginalis 'Purity'*;
    Snowflake, *P. x virginalis 'Minnesota Snowflake'*; Sweet,
    P. coronarius; Virginal, *P. x virginalis*
Mountain Ash: American, *Sorbus americana*; European,
    S. aucuparia
Mountain Heath, *Phyllodoce caerulea*
Mountain Laurel, *Kalmia latifolia*
Mulberry: Black (Common), *Morus nigra*; Weeping, *M. alba
    'pendula'*

Nannyberry, *Viburnum lentago*

Ninebark: Common, *Physocarpus opulifolius;* Dart's, *P. o. 'Dart's Gold'*; Golden, *P. o. 'luteus'*

Nut: Beaked Hazelnut, *Corylus cornuta;* Black Walnut, *Juglans nigra;* Butternut, *J. cineria;* Hazelnut, *Corylus avellana;* Heartnut, *J. sieboldiana 'cordiformis'*; Manchurian Walnut, *J. mandshurica*

Oak: English, *Quercus robur (Q. pendunculata)*; Pin, *Q. palustris;* Red, *Q. rubra (Q. borealis)*

Ohio Buckeye, *Aesculus glabra*

Partridgeberry (Two-Eyed Berry), *Mitchella repens*

Peach, *Prunus persica*

Pear, *Pyrus* spp.

Periwinkle, *Vinca minor*

Pieris: Lily-of-the-Valley, *Pieris japonica;* Mountain, *P. floribunda*

Pine: Austrian, *Pinus nigra;* Bristlecone, *P. aristata;* Dwarf Mugo, *P. mugo vars.*; Dwarf Scots, *P. sylvestris 'nana'*; (Eastern) White, *P. strobus;* Jack, *P. banksiana;* Korean, *P. koraiensis;* Pumilio Mugo, *P. mugo pumilio;* Red, *P. resinosa;* Scots, *P. sylvestris;* Swiss Stone, *P. cembra*

Poplar: Berlin, *Populus berolinensis;* Bolleana, *P. alba 'pyramidalis'*; Lombardy, *P. nigra 'Italica'*; Silver (White), *P. alba 'nivea'*

Privet: Amur (Lover's), *Ligustrum amurense;* Cheyenne, *L. vulgare 'Cheyenne'*; Common, *L. vulgare;* Golden (Vicary), *L. vulgare 'aureum'* or *P. 'Vicaryi'*; Ibolium, *L. x ibolium*

Quince: Common (Flowering), *Chaenomeles speciosa;* Edible (Common), *Cydonia oblonga;* Japanese, *Chaenomeles japonica*

Rhododendron: PJM, *Rhododendron x 'P.J. Mezzitt'*; Small-Leaved, *R. spp. and hybrids;* Various Sizes, *R. spp. and hybrids;* Wild (Rhodora), *R. canadense*

Rose: Shrub, *Rosa spp. and hybrids*

Rosemary, *Rosmarinus officinalis*

Rowan (European Mountain Ash), *Sorbus aucuparia*

Russian Olive, *Elaeagnus angustifolia*

Sage, *Salvia officinalis*
St. John's Wort, *Hypericum patulum 'Sungold'*
Sea Buckthorn: Common, *Hippophae rhamnoides*
Siberian (Chinese) Pear, *Pyrus ussuriensis*
Silver Lace Vine, *Polygonum aubertii*
Smoke Tree, *Cotinus coggygria*
Snowberry (Waxberry), *Symphoricarpos albus*
Spirea: Anthony Waterer, *Spirea x bumalda 'Anthony Waterer'*;
    Bridal Wreath, *S. x vanhouttei*; Bullata, *S. japonica 'Bullata'*;
    Garland, *S. x arguta*; Goldflame, *S. x bumalda 'Goldflame'*;
    Goldmound, *S. x bumalda 'Goldmound'*; Little Princess, *S. j.
    'Little Princess'*; Nana, *S. j. 'nana'*; Pink, *S. x billiardii or S.
    douglasii*; Snowmound, *S. nipponica 'Snowmound'*
Spruce: Bird's Nest, *Picea abies 'nidiformis'*; Colorado Blue, *P.
    pungens vars.*; Common (Norway), *P. abies (P. excelsa)*;
    Dwarf Alberta, *P. glauca albertiana 'conica'*; Dwarf Alberta
    Globe, *P. glauca albertiana 'conica' forma globosa*; Dwarf
    Blue, *P. pungens glauca vars.*; Ohlendorff, *P. abies
    'Ohlendorffii'*; Serbian, *P. omorika*; White (Canadian),
    P. glauca (P. alba)
Sumac: Chinese, *Rhus chinensis*; Staghorn, R. *typhina*;
    Dissecta, *R. t. 'dissecta'* incorrectly *'laciniata'*

Tamarix: Feathery, *Tamarix parviflora*; Five-Stamen, *T. ramo-
    sissima*
Thuja, *see Cedar*
Thyme: Creeping, *Thymus spp.*
Trumpet Vine, *Campsis radicans*
Tulip Tree, *Liriodendron tulipifera*

Viburnum: Burkwood, *Viburnum x burkwoodii*; (European)
    Snowball, *V. opulus 'roseum'*; Fragrant Snowball,
    V. x carlcephalum; Korean Spice, *V. carlesii*
Virginia Creeper, *Parthenocissus quinquefolia*

Wayfaring Tree, *Viburnum lantana*
Weigela, *Weigela spp. and hybrids*
Willow: Arctic (Basket), *Salix purpurea 'nana'* incorrectly
    'gracilis'; White, *S. alba*
Wintercreeper, *Euonymus fortunei 'coloratus'*

Wintergreen (Teaberry), *Gaultheria procumbens*
Wisteria, *Wisteria floribunda* and *W. sinensis*
Witch Hazel: Common, *Hamamelis virginiana*
Witherod, *Viburnum cassinoides*

Yew: Brown's, *Taxus x media 'Brownii'*; Canada (Ground
  Hemlock), *T. canadensis;* Dark Green, *T. x media 'Dark
  Green'*; Dense, *T. cuspidata 'densa'*; Dwarf Japanese, *T. cuspi-
  data 'nana'*; Hick's, *T. x media 'Hicksii'*; Hill's, *T. x media
  'Hillii'*; Upright Japanese, *T. cuspidata*
Yucca: Adam's Needle, *Yucca filamentosa;* Spanish Bayonet,
  Y. glauca

Zelkova (Japanese), *Zelkova serrata*

Index